RULERS AND CAPITAL
IN HISTORICAL PERSPECTIVE

RULERS AND CAPITAL IN HISTORICAL PERSPECTIVE

*State Formation and Financial Development
in India and the United States*

ABHISHEK CHATTERJEE

TEMPLE UNIVERSITY PRESS
Philadelphia • Rome • Tokyo

TEMPLE UNIVERSITY PRESS
Philadelphia, Pennsylvania 19122
www.temple.edu/tempress

Library of Congress Cataloging-in-Publication Data

Names: Chatterjee, Abhishek, 1977– author.
Title: Rulers and capital in historical perspective : state formation and
    financial development in India and the United States / Abhishek Chatterjee.
Description: Philadelphia : Temple University Press, [2017] | Includes
    bibliographical references and index.
Identifiers: LCCN 2017010535 (print) | LCCN 2017027115 (ebook) |
    ISBN 9781439915028 (e-book) | ISBN 9781439915004 (cloth : alk. paper)
Subjects: LCSH: Capital market—United States—18th century. | Capital
    market—India—History—18th century. | Capital market—United
    States—19th century. | Capital market—India—History—19th century.
Classification: LCC HG4963 (ebook) | LCC HG4963 .C43 2017 (print) |
    DDC 332/.04150973—dc23
LC record available at https://lccn.loc.gov/2017010535

Printed in the United States of America

9 8 7 6 5 4 3 2 1

Contents

Acknowledgments

THIS BOOK BEGAN ITS LIFE—as many such books do—as a dissertation. That it took over six years to develop into a book is a testament to my singular lack of discipline. That it actually became a book at all is evidence of my singular good fortune. What follows is an effort to both understand and enumerate at least some of this luck.

I learned a lot from John Echeverri-Gent, Mark Schwartz, and David Waldner at the University of Virginia even before they kindly agreed to direct my dissertation. They prompted me to ask some fundamental questions about the social world and the nature of the social sciences. They bear no responsibility for the intellectual detours that followed, since they gave me fair warning about the potential consequences of pursuing these questions. I thank them for being inspirational mentors and for having high standards. I can only hope that I have succeeded in meeting at least some of their expectations.

Shamira Gelbman has edited almost everything I have published so far, including a couple of chapters in this book. Her efforts have shielded readers from my (sometimes more than) occasional flights into prolixity and overexplanation. She gave me her editorial help in addition to sixteen years of friendship (since we first took a class together in

2001) and commiseration. She did not, alas, edit this Acknowledgments section.

Discussions with Jason Brownlee and Ellis Goldberg have been vital sources of intellectual nourishment, especially when preoccupation with my own project might have caused me to lose sight of debates and discussions in many other areas of the discipline. I thank them for including me in their conversations and for extending their hospitality to me on more than a few occasions. I also thank Ryan Saylor and Rudy Sil, who—despite their busy schedules—repeatedly responded to my requests for professional counsel.

My colleagues in the Political Science Department at the University of Montana provided a congenial environment for developing my dissertation into a book. They were unfailingly supportive and kind at a time when I was finding my feet in a new job and a brand-new place. I thank Karen Adams, Ramona Grey, Paul Haber, and Chris Muste for lending me a sympathetic ear and offering advice on numerous occasions. Jeff Green was always available for an entertaining chat, especially about his experiences as a southerner in the West. Peter Koehn took me ice fishing, which, I learned, is not one of my favorite activities. One of the pleasures of my new job was reconnecting with my graduate school classmate Rob Saldin, who was, and continues to be, a good friend and confidant.

I am fortunate that this manuscript landed in the hands of Aaron Javsicas, editor-in-chief at Temple University Press, who more than made up for my lack of efficiency by guiding me through the publication process remarkably swiftly. I also thank him for seeking out especially perspicacious reviewers, whose comments have certainly improved the book. I thank the anonymous reviewers for their close reading of the manuscript and for their insightful suggestions. Profuse thanks are also due to Joan Vidal, senior production editor, and Rose Elfman, copyeditor, for guiding me through the different stages of the production process and for making the book more readable than it otherwise would have been.

A slightly modified version of Chapter 4 was previously published as Abhishek Chatterjee, "Financial Property Rights under Colonialism: Some Counterfactual Possibilities," *Journal of Institutional Eco-*

nomics 12, no. 4 (2016): 797–824. I thank Geoffrey Hodgson, the editor of that journal, for permission to republish the article. Several chapters of this book were also presented at various conferences. I thank Richard Bensel, Daniel Carpenter, Jason Jackson, and Elizabeth Sanders for their comments and suggestions on these occasions.

Though writing this book, beginning with the dissertation, was a fulfilling experience, it was not necessarily a pleasurable one. Although it may not have been their intention, my friends made me realize that the world did not care a whit whether I wrote a book. This was a strangely comforting thought—an example of Bertrand Russell's proposition that "nothing that happens to oneself is of any cosmic importance"—that has sustained me for long periods of time.[1] It may surprise Jackson Bunch, Matt Fry, Karl Mangold, Maria Mangold, and Daisy Rooks that their friendship over the past five years helped lead me to this conclusion. It would probably not surprise Brent Ryckman, however, given our many discussions about such issues; I look forward to our continuing conversation about the nature of human existence, interspersed with musings about the nature of science (Brent is allegedly a good virologist; I say this to get even with him for gently mocking the social "sciences"). Rebecca Yurman, who witnessed the writing of my dissertation, has my sympathy.

It might be considered a mistake to ascribe certain kinds of intentionality to nonhuman animals. I'm convinced, however, that though Kenny did not intend to help me with my writing, he did intend to wake me up each morning to demand affection and then greet me at the door at the end of each day. He died, quite suddenly, shortly after I signed the contract to publish this book—almost as if to indicate that his job here was done. Though Kenny wouldn't have cared, I dedicate this book to him and to all my fellow humans' feline companions.

Finally, I dedicate this book to my mom and dad, Krishna and Amitava Chatterjee, whose love and support—sometimes from thousands of miles away—has made most things in my life possible.

A.C.
December 2, 2016
Missoula, MT

Rulers and Capital in Historical Perspective

1

Introduction

The Question and the Argument in Brief

The same confidence which disposes great merchants and manu-facturers, upon ordinary occasions, to trust their property to the protection of a particular government, disposes them, upon extra-ordinary occasions, to trust that government with the use of their property. By lending money to government, they do not even for a moment diminish their ability to carry on their trade and manu-factures. On the contrary, they commonly augment it. The neces-sities of the state render government upon most occasions willing to borrow upon terms extremely advantageous to the lender. The security which it grants to the original creditor is made transferable to any other creditor, and, from the universal confidence in the justice of the state, generally sells in the market for more than was originally paid for it. The merchant or monied man makes money by lending money to government, and instead of diminishing, increases his trading capital.

—**ADAM SMITH**, *THE WEALTH OF NATIONS*

National debts, *i.e.*, the alienation of the state—whether despotic, constitutional or republican—marked with its stamp the capitalis-tic era. The only part of the so-called national wealth that actually enters into the collective possessions of modern peoples is their national debt. Hence, as a necessary consequence, the modern doctrine that a nation becomes the richer the more deeply it is in debt. Public credit becomes the *credo* of capital. And with the rise of national debt-making, want of faith in the national debt takes the place of the blasphemy against the Holy Ghost, which may not be forgiven. . . . The state creditors actually give nothing away, for the sum lent is transformed into public bonds, easily negotiable, which go on functioning in their hands just as so much hard cash would. . . . At their birth the great banks, decorated with national titles, were only associations of private speculators, who placed themselves by the side of governments, and, thanks to the privileges they received, were in a position to advance money to the State.

—KARL MARX, *CAPITAL*

Concentration of money in banks, though not the sole cause, is the principal cause which has made the money market of England so exceedingly rich, so much beyond other countries.

—WALTER BAGEHOT, *LOMBARD STREET*

SPANNING ABOUT A HUNDRED YEARS, and representing somewhat different normative perspectives, the quotes above describe two closely related phenomena: the emergence of tradable public debt and the rise of private money and credit markets. The phenomena are related because both were based fundamentally on, in Smith's words, "the universal confidence in the justice of the state." The state was responsible for enforcing impersonal contracts, both between it and investors and among traders and other participants, and it was this role that was the subject of "universal confidence": in other words, the relationship between the state and investors was *institutionalized* in the sense that it was ultimately based on stable mutual expectations between the two parties. This state of affairs facilitated, among other things, the emergence of deposit banking on a large scale. Additionally, the fact that the state became implicated in guaranteeing the security of "public" credit and in being an arbiter and contract enforcer in the "private" money market necessarily created a direct link between the two. This form of institutionalization distinguishes markets of the kind that Adam Smith and Karl Marx describe from markets and networks in commercial paper per se predating the emergence of national states.[1]

Some of the characteristics of banking and credit systems without any state involvement—that is, in the absence of state-enforced rules and regulations—can be illustrated by considering the *hundi*, a particular kind of financial instrument that was in use throughout the Indian subcontinent during the eighteenth and nineteenth centuries and whose origins date back to at least the sixteenth century. This was a bill of exchange issued by merchant-bankers that was used extensively to finance endeavors such as long-distance trade. Merchants would discount each other's *hundis*, and hence make payments (including for insurance) and more generally adjust their obligations using this instrument.[2] In this way the *hundi* functioned as both a credit instrument and a medium of payment, but its circulation was limited to merchant-banker networks. Similarly, it was also the case that bankers (*sarrafs*) would accept money deposits and grant interest on them, which, in turn, led to the creation of credit money.[3] But what such deposits created was fundamentally private money inasmuch as their acceptance was completely predicated on bankers' reputations among merchants, who were generally the chief depositors, and as a result they circulated only among specific networks.

Indeed, networks are limited by their very nature in the sense that those outside them cannot avail themselves of the relationships (of exchange or any other kind of transaction) that constitute them. Yet such networks can be incorporated into the state when it provides explicit and *institutionalized* backing. This does not mean that the networks cease to exist: rather, they begin to function within the overarching context of impersonal rules that the state enforces. The legal backing of the state is what gives credit and banking their public character. To the extent that networks such as the ones described above existed outside the purview of the legal structure of the state, they could be called informal, to contrast with the formal state involvement implied in the chapter epigraphs.

To return to Adam Smith's quote, why is it that "the universal confidence in the justice of the state" occurred in only a small number of now developed countries during the eighteenth and early nineteenth centuries (including England and the United States)? Notwithstanding their substantial mercantile capital, a vast majority of emerging states, both independent and colonial, lacked these structures. For instance, despite the presence of an extensive class of merchant-bankers who traded in a variety of credit instruments and who were often creditors to British and other European merchants over the seventeenth and eighteenth centuries, neither precolonial nor colonial India would quite fit the description in the previous paragraph. Modern models of explicitly state-endorsed and state-supported money and credit markets did not exist in precolonial India, while the colonial period was characterized by a dichotomy between an informal—albeit substantial—native money and credit market and a formal, though severely limited, European market.

The association between certain kinds of state involvement and financial development (or, alternatively, modernization) should not be surprising for two related reasons. First, in the words of Richard Sylla, Richard Tilly, and Gabriel Tortella, "Long before private economic entities . . . came to require financing on a scale beyond the capabilities of individual proprietors and partners, governments had needs for large-scale finance."[4] State involvement consequently has the capacity to bring together large numbers of financial capital holders. Second, this, in turn, has the potential to facilitate the further development of impersonal state-enforced rules, since the network system on its own would not be able to sustain itself beyond a certain number of participants. Impersonal rules backed by state coercion can further facilitate the growth of such a system by increasing the numbers of people involved.

Given the significance of modern financial systems to subsequent industrial revolutions in states where such systems did develop—something that has not gone unnoticed in the economic history literature—the causes of their emergence are certainly worth investigating.[5] Attributing the poor development of financial systems to colonialism would seem to beg the question. Why should colonialism retard market development, especially since it is often credited with introducing European-style market institutions in the first place?[6] Also, this explanation does not account for the lack of an institutionalized financial system during the period immediately preceding colonization. But if, as according to Smith, "the same confidence which disposes great merchants and manufacturers . . . to trust their property to the protection of a particular government, disposes them, upon extraordinary occasions, to trust that government with the use of their property," an interrogation of sources of "confidence in the justice of the state" would seem to be a more promising beginning. Specifically, what were the conditions that enabled confidence? What did such conditions entail, and how and why, exactly, did they promote confidence?

The preceding questions—albeit in the context of property in general—have motivated much of the modern literature on property rights, which has linked economic growth to governmental protection of such rights.[7] The general framework may be stated as follows. Rulers provide protection or guarantee property rights (for their constituents) in return for payment or other resource assistance. But they also have the incentive to renege on their end of the implicit bargain by seizing property. The larger this probability, the less likely capital holders are to invest in the economy; lower levels of aggregate investment then result in underdevelopment.

Applied to financial systems, therefore, this property rights argument contends that although thriving debt and credit markets constitute an important financial resource that is advantageous to the state, such markets could not have a stable existence if participants do not expect rulers to carry out their end of the bargain. This includes expecting the state to honor debts—for example, by not unilaterally depreciating them—and not to seize or otherwise damage financial wealth. It follows that variation in the stability of financial systems can be explained by variation in the state's demonstrated willingness and ability to uphold financial compacts. Yet, assuming that both rulers and financial capital holders are rational egoists, creating and maintaining this expectation is no easy task.[8] As Douglass C. North and Barry R. Weingast argue, it is difficult even if there has been a history of interaction between rulers/states and investors, since rulers could always heavily discount the future (or the possibility of profitable future interactions) for a variety of reasons.[9]

The difficulty of creating stable expectations arises fundamentally from the fact that the preferences of the state and of the investors are independent of each other. But an arrangement that could somehow align their preferences, making them interdependent, would seem to largely mitigate the problem. Such an arrangement would be self-enforcing in the sense that neither party would have the incentive to unilaterally deviate from it (since deviating would entail unacceptable costs for both sides). Moreover, whatever the specific institutional form of this arrangement, it would also perforce be independent of the specific identities and interests of the individuals or groups involved. Indeed, the preferences of individuals or groups occupying certain institutional spaces could even be seen as partially endogenous to, or an outcome of, such arrangements. For all of the reasons underlined above, such an arrangement would constitute what North and Weingast term a "credible commitment" to potential investors.

North and Weingast base their argument on the case of England, where a formal public credit system and a money market emerged at the same time as the institutionalization of parliamentary supremacy and the establishment of a judiciary independent of the Crown. They therefore argue that these two innovations were parts of a credible commitment to investors, since they greatly constricted the ability of the Crown to act unilaterally against the interests of investors and creditors. A third institutional change they identify as part of this commitment was the incorporation of creditors into the state through the Bank of England, whose function, among other things, was to handle the government's accounts. Moreover, the bank's notes were backed by the government. Together, these developments constituted a commitment to investors (or creditors) because the government had essentially turned its payment functions over to its creditors in such a way that any failure to make interest payments would have constricted its ability to make payments for other purposes.[10]

The following chapter argues that this third constraint, rather than—as some have assumed—the other two, was crucial to the credibility of the commitment made by the state. It suffices here to observe that although such institutional commitments can greatly mitigate the problem of reneging on a pact, their very provenance requires explanation. Such commitments entail substantial costs in terms of restriction on one's (in this instance, the state's) freedom, essentially precluding courses of action that would otherwise be available. If both parties to a costly agreement are rationally egoistic (a usual assumption in the literature), it seems unlikely that one of them would be willing to bear most of the immediate costs of that agreement. Given these conditions, it becomes difficult to see how such an agreement would have emerged in the first place.

Put somewhat differently, under what conditions would one of the (rationally egoist) parties to an interaction make concessions that would seem to go against its immediate interest but that could result in the development of modern financial systems in the long run? The answer I advance in this book is that rulers were forced to make institutional concessions only when local merchants or financiers as a group became their only major resource for financing their activities. However, this did not happen often, either because land revenue tended to predominate as a source of financing or because, as tended to be true for many colonial situations, rulers could utilize foreign money and credit markets that had already emerged. The next chapter represents this kind of interaction as a bargaining situation between two rationally egoist groups where one (the rulers) had an advantage over the other (financial capital holders). These situations tended to be singularly uncongenial for the emergence of the kinds of institutionalized and integrated financial systems described above.

Thus, local merchants and bankers were not institutionally incorporated into the state either under the Mughal Empire (which derived the bulk of its revenues from taxes on land) or subsequently under the East India Company or the British state (both of which raised substantial capital from the London financial market). Indeed, although Sir James Steuart, the famous eighteenth-century economist and consultant to the East India Company, advised that the state should incorporate indigenous bankers and financiers in this way, the Company did not follow his recommendation—as the argument of this book would have predicted.

Despite many other contextual differences, the situation in the North American colonies prior to independence was fundamentally similar in that their reliance on the London market precluded the development of formal financial institutions. The Revolutionary War disrupted existing financial arrangements, and the exigencies of financing it led to the development of an institutionalized financial system connected to the state. As subsequent chapters show, taxes on land and property were far from sufficient to meet the requirements of the fledgling government. Colonial merchants were the sole group who were both able and willing to meet the state's financial needs. However, rulers had to assure them that their investment in the new state was secure. It was these efforts that entailed the institutional innovations that were a part of a credible commitment, referred to earlier. In contrast to the situation in India, North American rulers did not hold a bargaining advantage over financial capital holders and hence were willing to make credible institutional commitments.

A second part of my argument in this book concerns the effects of such commitments on the subsequent politics of market development. The very establishment of these institutions in the United States gave investors as a group both a common interest and the means of defending it. It gave them tangible and specific status quo positions to defend:

any policy move that enhanced the government's ability to *unilaterally* repudiate or devalue debt would unite investors in opposition. In addition, given the institutional set-up by that point, any step back toward the situation that existed prior to the emergence of an institutionalized and integrated money and credit system would have jeopardized the economy's entire system of payments, in the process also harming the government and many others. Thus, as Chapter 5 demonstrates, bankers and financiers were united in their opposition to policies that had the potential to increase direct and unilateral government influence over the total stock of payment medium (as well as over the question of what counted as such) in the economy.[11] For instance, despite their variant party affiliations and differing opinions on other policy questions, they were united in their opposition to any proposal that allowed the federal government to directly own banks. As some of them pointed out at the time, any such move would have damaged the government's credibility in the eyes of investors, thereby potentially endangering a substantial section of the economy. And even Andrew Jackson discovered that he would have to abandon his plan to replace the Bank of the United States with a bank founded on the federal government's credit if he was going to retain allies and succeed in his campaign to prevent the Bank from renewing its federal charter.

Yet the fact that Jackson succeeded in his battle against the Bank of the United States also indicates another phenomenon. In the context of an already existing institutionalized financial system, rulers or executives can have considerable freedom of action vis-à-vis investors and financiers as long as some of the system's basic institutional features remain unaffected. In practice, this translates to the freedom to propose policies that, rather than uniting capital holders in opposition, are likely to divide them by having differential impacts on various groups of financial investors. As the history of the first and second Banks of the United States demonstrates, relevant groups of people were implicitly aware of the importance of depicting policy measures as either injurious or irrelevant to vital institutional features of the financial system and hence to financial capital holders as a whole.[12] Supporters of the two Banks would try to portray them as linchpins of the entire banking and financial system and therefore beneficial to all investors, while opponents would retort that the Banks were irrelevant at best (and harmful at worst) to the interests of investors as a whole and that they unfairly advantaged one subset of financiers over all others.

As the next few chapters demonstrate, focusing on the emergence of credible commitments not only helps to account for the emergence of modern, institutionalized money and credit systems; it also makes sense of many aspects of the politics that such institutions actuate. Thus, it helps to explain the policy proposals, conflicts, and changes that subsequently occur within these systems. For instance, comprehending the origins of the United States' financial system also illuminates the nature of the struggle over the two Banks of the United States and the progressive lowering of entry barriers to banking during the first third of the nineteenth century.

This book is organized as follows. The next chapter delineates its theoretical framework, explaining how the emergence of modern, state-connected money markets was the result of a certain kind of power relationship between rulers and financial capital holders that forced the two groups to cooperate and how certain kinds of financial systems represented the institutionalization of this cooperation. In doing so, this chapter provides a definition of power that explains how it can influence the incentives of otherwise rationally egoist actors or groups to cooperate with one another. The chapter also considers alternative arguments about the specific institutions that demonstrate credible commitment, arguing that one strand of the literature has identified such institutions incorrectly. It then discusses other explanations for the developments in the U.S. money and credit market during the first third of the nineteenth century, including the establishment and demise of the two Banks of the United States. While the argument I proffer can accommodate explanations that highlight the role of non-egoistic motivations in policy outcomes, this chapter points out that such explanations remain incomplete or inadequate if they do not account for relative bargaining power, and hence the nature of existing institutions (since extant institutional rules affect relative bargaining power). It further observes that assessing the role of bargaining power implies considering how egoistic (or gain-seeking) motivations interact with nonegoistic (or, loosely stated, ideological) ones. The chapter concludes with a discussion of the methodology used in this book, including the issue of empirically substantiating counterfactual propositions.[13]

Chapter 3 explains the lack of capital markets in the North American colonies by tracing this to an asymmetric power relationship: the relationship of dependence between colonial merchants and their British creditors. It demonstrates why it was rarely in the interests of either the capital holders of the metropole or the rulers who depended on them to allow the formation of a local capital market. This chapter then explains the emergence of a state-connected capital market in the aftermath of the American Revolution, showing that the war put an end to the dependency that had inhibited such a system.

Chapter 4 offers a sketch of the situation in India under the later Mughal rulers and accounts for the lack of an *institutionalized* cooperative relationship between these rulers and the substantial commercial and mercantile community of the subcontinent. This chapter then explains why the advent of the British East India Company state also precluded the emergence of a formal state-connected capital market. Here it considers one notable juncture, very early in the period of Company rule, when cooperation with indigenous capital holders and the Company state could have been institutionalized: while this was indeed contemplated, it was eventually rejected by the Company state because, owing to its superior bargaining position, the Company could disregard the interests of native financial capital holders.

Chapter 5 comes back to the United States to explain subsequent developments in the money market, especially its changing structure. Here, my major objective is to account for the gradual lowering of the market's entry barriers, culminating with the Jackson administration's refusal to renew the charter for the second Bank of the United States.

Chapter 6 concludes by considering other cases where the theoretical framework elaborated in this book might apply and exploring the further implications of various arguments concerning the lack of economic development in certain colonies. In particular, it casts some doubts on arguments that link institutional features like property-rights protections and limited government to long-term economic growth. These doubts arise in part because the specific institutions that the literature identifies as important, such as a legislative body and a judiciary independent of the executive, may not have had the powers attributed to them.

2

The Argument
and the Literature(s)

ON THE INSTITUTIONS
OF "CREDIBLE COMMITMENT"

NORTH AND WEINGAST'S ARGUMENT about credible commitments and the development of public and private credit places considerable emphasis on the fact that the emergence of an institutionalized financial system in England was associated with the establishment of Parliamentary supremacy and a judiciary independent of the Crown. This association is partly due to the role of such bodies in restricting unilateral executive action: they make it very difficult for the executive to enact measures without consulting the other groups affected by such measures and taking their preferences into account. Additionally, insofar as North and Weingast's argument implies that these political and financial institutions emerged from causes unrelated to each other, the former could be considered exogenous to the latter.

In one strand of the literature on financial systems, these theoretical assumptions form the basis of the claim that Anglo-American-style limited governments exogenously facilitate the establishment of stable and efficient financial systems. So, for instance, Stephen Haber, Armando Razo, and Noel Maurer argue that the first and best guarantor of such a financial system is a limited government of the kind exemplified by the United States and the United Kingdom, because it acts as a credible commitment to investors.[1]

Yet North and Weingast's argument also allows another interpretation. This second interpretation suggests that first, the institutions of "credible commitment" were endogenous, and second—once their endogeneity to other factors, such as coalitions and power relationships is established—the *specific* institutions of limited government were epiphenomenal to said factors; the co-occurrence of institutions of limited government with the development of an institutionalized financial system was an artifact of the historical conditions of seventeenth-century England.

Their statement that they sought to "explain the evolution of political institutions in seventeenth-century England, focusing on the fundamental institutions of representative government emerging out of the Glorious Revolution of 1688" suggests that their argument did not imply that these institutions developed exogenously.[2] Furthermore, credible commitments need not include such features as elected, independent legislatures and party competition based on broad electoral suffrage. The English case is a bit deceptive on this count, but certain attributes of its institutions of credible commitment precisely illustrate why it was not limited government per se but rather the coalitions and power relationships behind these institutions that accounted for their outcomes.

In England, the credible commitment included the institutionalization of parliamentary supremacy and a judiciary independent of the Crown. But this worked only because of particular historical circumstances. Governmental commitment was directed toward a very specific class of wealth holders, who constituted the Parliament.[3] Throughout the eighteenth century and for the first third of the nineteenth, the franchise was highly restricted in England. This meant that the major wealth holders or investors had disproportionate influence on state policy relative to, say, workers or peasants. Political contestation was limited to certain parameters or certain issues—namely, those over which the (restricted) membership of the Parliament disagreed. Thus, as long as parliamentary membership was limited in this manner, the institution was a very effective commitment to the interests of investors. It could not possibly be expected to perform similarly once the franchise was expanded to include all classes of individuals.

The example above exposes one of the problems with the argument that a limited government allows investors to mobilize and assert their interests through an independent legislature in ways that constrict the executive's freedom of action. By the same logic, universal adult suffrage should also allow those disadvantaged by the banking system in general, as well as those opposed to banking *qua* business (as opposed to a public service), to organize against major investors and advance policies that might violate the initial commitment. The obvious point here is that this particular form of commitment is "credible" only when investor interests are necessarily *and* overwhelmingly represented in formal political institutions and hence in public politics. England's Parliament in the seventeenth and eighteenth centuries could fulfill this role, but as the historical situation changed, some other institutional form would have to replace it or the commitment would break down.

The importance of the specific composition of the Parliament has not gone unremarked in the literature. David Stasavage has argued that partisan control of "veto points" such as the Parliament in England had a relatively large influence on credible commitments to investors.[4] Without the right kind of partisan control, he contends, a commitment to repay debts would not be credible because an ideologically hostile majority could always rescind the debts along with the institutional privileges accorded to the Bank of England. He further shows evidence that Whig control correlated with lower costs of borrowing for the government.[5] Thus, he concludes that partisan preferences were more important than institutional commitments.

Yet Stasavage's argument does not quite imply that partisan control by itself was necessary: such control would explain only very short-term credibility, and under conditions particular to eighteenth-century England. If the population's median preferences were to coincide with the Parliamentary median, due perhaps to a broadening of the electorate and the removal of franchise restrictions (indeed, Stasavage's arguments depend on a gap between the median preferences of the two groups), the credibility of the government's commitments would tend to break down. The important point here is that such commitments cannot be seen as self-reinforcing.[6]

Why, then, did the commitment in England not break down with the expansion of suffrage in the nineteenth century? The answer can be found in North and Weingast's argument, which points out that Parliament was not the only institution of credible commitment. The other one was the Bank of England, which was basically an incorporation of the subscribers to a large government loan.

> The Bank was responsible for handling the loan accounts of the government and for assuring the continuity of promised distributions. . . . As [Thomas] Macaulay observed . . . since loans to the Crown went through the Bank, "it must have instantly stopped payment if it had ceased to receive the interest on the sum which it had advanced to the government." The government had thus created an additional, private constraint on its future behavior by making it difficult to utilize funds of current loans if it failed to honor its previous obligations.[7]

The importance of this constraint cannot be gainsaid: indeed, it was crucial to sustaining the original governmental commitment as historical situations changed.

It is this latter constraint—in various other guises in different times and places—that, in the long term, partially shields the interests of investors from the vagaries of politics. For without this severing of the direct link between politics and certain matters of economic or financial policy, there would be nothing to stop organized opposition from enacting policies that could jeopardize any commitment that the government made.[8] It is worth reiterating that institutional arrangements that can restrict general public participation in certain issues are self-reinforcing inasmuch as deviation from such arrangements can adversely affect not only the interests of the state but also, collaterally, large parts of the economy. This means that even if subsequent expansion of suffrage dilutes investor interests in the legislatures of limited governments, the costs to the economy or even to the state could deter otherwise hostile legislators from enacting policies that could affect aspects of credible commitments adversely. In other words, the preferences of legislators could become endogenous to such commitments.[9] There is no reason, therefore, why this private constraint could also not operate in regimes or governments that are not limited, because it is in principle separable from other narrowly political institutions. Indeed, the nature of such institutions becomes irrelevant to the credibility of the commitment in this case.

The self-enforcing nature of the credible commitment is therefore crucial to its success, and the institutions of limited government are neither exogenous nor self-enforcing in the sense described above. In fact, every argument made ostensibly to demonstrate the relative instability (and inefficiency) of other institutional arrangements also applies with equal force to Anglo-American-style limited governments. The endogeneity of political institutions to power relations blurs the supposedly clear distinction between them.

For example, Haber, Razo, and Maurer argue that in the absence of a limited government, alternative institutional arrangements for commitments may develop but cannot deliver long-term stability or efficiency. Because of their sensitivity to a variety of contextual factors, these institutions tend to be sporadic and lack the same degree of credibility.[10] Using the case of Mexico, the authors point to one such institutional arrangement, which they call a vertically politically integrated (VPI) coalition, in order to demonstrate its vulnerability to factors such as the government's rate of time discount.[11] Yet, as argued above, the same should apply to the political institutions of limited government. There are no theoretical reasons for expecting limited governments to be conducive to financial development, and, as a corollary, there are no theoretical reasons for expecting authoritarian regimes to be unable to make effective institutional commitments that promote the establishment of stable financial systems. Indeed, the converse also holds: the commitment problems that, in the absence of limited government, VPI coalitions are supposed to mitigate are also endemic to limited governments. In other words, key attributes of VPI coalitions do not really distinguish them from the supposedly better Anglo-American-style governments.

This becomes clearer with Haber, Razo, and Maurer's description of one aspect of VPI coalitions, which borrows from work on vertically integrated firms:

> If information asymmetries between two firms are high, then firm A can never be certain whether firm B is behaving opportunistically, or is just trying to renegotiate the contract because of events beyond its control. Under these circumstances, vertical integration between two firms can reduce the incentives for opportunistic behavior because information asymmetries are lower within a single, merged firm than between two separate ones. Obviously, it is not possible for a government and an asset holder to form a "firm." It is possible, however, for the line between the government and private asset holders to become blurred—so blurred, in fact, that as a practical matter it is difficult to distinguish precisely where the government ends and the asset holders begin. . . . Governments may ask private bodies to write policies or the heads of the government's executive agencies might be drawn from the most prominent asset holders in the country.[12]

Although somewhat vague, this description could be applied to the institutional situations under the first and second Banks of the United States, the Bank of England, the Dutch Republic during the seventeenth and eighteenth centuries, and numerous other financial systems with independent central banks in putatively limited governments. Moreover, the fact that it applies to all of these cases makes a lot of theoretical sense. As argued above, enforcement problems are not mitigated under Anglo-American-style governments just because an independent judiciary and a parliament apparently limit the executive branch. The same holds for information asymmetries. Indeed, electoral competition with broad suffrage can introduce new actors and variables to the polity that tend to exacerbate information asymmetries between governments and private asset holders. The problem, again, is the misidentification of institutions of credible commitment, or alternatively the misattribution of this commitment to institutions that were adventitious to the emergence of actual (self-enforcing) institutions of credible commitment.

THE THEORETICAL ARGUMENT

Explaining the Emergence of Institutionalized Money and Credit Systems

The emergence of institutions of credible commitment remains to be explained, however. North and Weingast's work does not focus on the origins of such arrangements as much as on their implication in the emergence of an institutionalized financial system as a whole. In their explanation, certain institutions solve the problem of possible government defection from the compact by preventing it from acting unilaterally. Yet the conditions under which a government would accede to such an arrangement are not specified. Indeed, if the situation between the government and asset holders or investors is akin to a prisoners' dilemma to begin with, such institutional arrangements would seem unlikely to ever emerge.

This problem led North in his subsequent work to worry about "third party enforcement in contracting," particularly "the development of the state as a coercive force able to monitor property rights and enforce contracts effectively"; as noted above, "with a strictly wealth-maximizing behavioral assumption it is hard even to create such a model abstractly."[13] As we shall see, the explanation I offer below does not require the state to be a neutral arbiter, thus circumventing North's problem. In fact, the question of the state being neutral—at least when it comes to the development of institutionalized money and credit systems—does not even arise in the same way: "neutral" has little analytical meaning in the context of a bargaining situation between rulers and financial capital holders, since the very institutional rules (that the state is supposed to be neutral toward) are not distributionally neutral from a societal perspective. Loosely stated, the consequences of rules, in terms of who gains (or loses), are not the same for everybody. The question, rather, is whether an institutional pact between the state and financial capital holders may be possible.

It is still possible, however, to account for such arrangements within a decidedly rationalist framework once, in addition to abandoning the exchange set-up, where parties exchange one good (protection) for another (financial resources), we relax one of the assumptions implicit in such a framework—namely, that the parties to the negotiation are necessarily equals.[14] Indeed, as I argue, power differentials sufficiently—though not necessarily—determine the structure of interaction and hence the incentive of the respective parties to mutually cooperate. The following section therefore provides a theoretical account of the sufficient conditions that allow for the emergence of credible commitments, which in turn result in the emergence of institutionalized financial systems.

Jack Knight conceptualizes power as the ability of one group or person "to affect by some means the alternatives available to . . . [another] person or group."[15] The sources of this asymmetry could be differences in resource endowments between groups or even differences in institutional location. Indeed, asymmetry of resources can be directly translated into institutional asymmetry, inasmuch as those having resource advantages can create institutions that further solidify their initial advantage. In both instances asymmetry implies that in a bargaining situation between two actors or groups, the more powerful group has more or better alternatives (to a mutually successful bargain) than the less powerful individual or group.[16] The same situation can also be described as the more powerful group depending less on the weaker one than the weaker one depends on it.[17]

As Charles Tilly has noted concerning the formation of European states, rulers' viability relied on cooperation from "others who held the essential resources . . . and were reluctant to surrender them without strong pressure or compensation."[18] Investors and other financial wealth holders such as merchants and bankers could obviously be one such source, but rulers could have had other options, such as taxation or rents from ownership of land or other revenue-producing assets. Other things being equal, rulers would have an advantage over investors in any negotiation to the extent that they have access to multiple alternative sources of financial resources. However, this is only one aspect of the situation.

In a world where physical violence exists and can be deployed in a goal-directed manner, having force on one's side could be very useful for economic activities. Indeed, those who are supported by force would have a distinct advantage in commercial transactions. Insofar as rulers try to concentrate, even monopolize, the means of organized violence, their support could prove crucial in determining the profitability of any business activity. This would give investors an advantage to the extent that they had access to multiple rulers.

We can now go back to North and Weingast's framework and ask under what kind of bargaining or power situation rulers would be compelled to make the concessions (or pay the costs) required for the institutionalization of a financial system. Suppose that rulers had access to multiple sources of revenue and resources (such as land, ownership of rent-producing resources, and foreign borrowing) and local investors were faced with only one set of rulers, or potential rulers. The rulers, having the advantage in the relationship, would—again, *necessarily*—have little incentive to make binding institutional commitments that permanently impinge on their freedom of action vis-à-vis the economy.[19] Under these circumstances, rulers' variable discount rates or changes in rulers, among other idiosyncratic factors, are likely to create major problems for the continuing existence and stability of financial markets.[20]

Many colonial relationships, though not all, constitute a special case of this situation. In such relationships, foreign (inasmuch as the word "colonial" connotes "nonnative") rulers' independence from native investors is predicated on their access to foreign financial investors, land revenue, or control of rent-producing or extractable resources (or all of these). This situation is not conducive to the institutionalization of the kind of relationship between rulers and (native or domestic) investors that leads to the formation of a state-supported financial system. As I demonstrate with India, a corollary of this is that the state strengthens the property rights of landholders and/or binds itself institutionally to foreign creditors in an effort to maintain access to foreign capital markets in a way that is often detrimental to the interests of native or domestic financial capital holders.

Rulers, on the other hand, would need to bid for the support of domestic investors if their primary source of resources depended on the activities of this group (domestic merchants and bankers, for instance). Merchants and bankers, on their part, would be more likely to support rulers who better protected their interests (in cases where more than one group of potential rulers is available). Instead of an exchange, the relationship between rulers and financial capital holders would be more akin to one of coordination, wherein each party is better off cooperating when the other one does because not cooperating would directly harm its own interests.[21] Cooperation could take several forms, but each side would have an incentive to take steps that would make cooperation by the other more likely.

Why would this be the case? Why wouldn't each party automatically assume that the other party would also cooperate? The main reason is that one-sided adherence to the agreement might still be costlier than mutual cooperation. Each side would be uncertain of the other's intent, and it is quite possible that cooperation would not take place in the first round of interaction. On the other hand, if we consider the interaction between the two groups to be continuous rather than discrete and one-off—a far more realistic assumption—cooperation would become more likely as the actors learned from previous failures. Under such circumstances, rulers would have incentives to assure capital holders that they could recover, and possibly augment, their wealth by cooperating, while merchants and bankers would have an incentive to assure rulers of their own cooperation in maintaining rulers' external autonomy and internal hierarchy.

The institutional manifestation of such a mutual assurance could include versions of the "private" constraint discussed by North and Weingast. Such constraints have the capacity not only to convey a credible commitment of state intentions but also to insulate the interests of financial capital holders from those of other societal groups that might not have the same incentive structure as those of the rulers. An especially effective commitment is to transfer control of parts of the economy, especially those having to do with money and credit, to private banks, which would basically be an agglomeration of investors. The notes of such banks could be made acceptable for taxes and other payments in the economy or even accorded the status of currency. In this way private financial organizations would have privileged influence over the total stock of money in the economy. As discussed earlier, such private constraints developed a public face in the form of parliamentary supremacy in England, but that was due solely to the contextual fact that those claiming to assert control over purse strings also were the only ones who could vote and be elected to a legislature.

In a different historical context, such as the twentieth century, versions of the private constraint could also include the institution of a central bank independent of direct legislative control—precisely illustrating the impermanence of such a contextual condition—with power over monetary policy. Additional steps could include the ones North and Weingast describe: lenders handling state accounts and revenue receipts. Doing these things would further give both groups a stake in the maintenance of such a system: while investors would develop a concern for the profitability of the loans advanced, governing elites would have a similar preference for maintaining the solvency of the banks.

Taken together, such institutional commitments would be particularly propitious for the development of a market for state debts, since banks would be both underwriters for and investors in such debt. Insinuation of the state in the emergence of such markets would also perforce lead to the development of private money markets. As North and Weingast note in the context of England:

> The institutions leading to the growth of a stable market for public debt provided a large and positive externality for the parallel development of a market for private debt. Shortly after its formation for intermediating public debt, the Bank of England began private operations. Numerous other banks also began operations at this time. This development provided the institutional structure for pooling the savings of many individuals and for intermediation between borrowers and lenders. A wide range of securities and negotiable instruments emerged in the early eighteenth century and these were used to finance a large range of activities.[22]

This progression is not surprising, since the institutional commitments described above decisively implicate the state in market transactions; indeed, the market becomes constituted by such institutions. The state's commitment to institutional rules translates over time to confidence in its commitment to enforcing impersonal contracts (consistent with these rules), such enforcement being crucial to the development of mass deposit banking. It is precisely this state of affairs that both Smith and Marx implied in the quotes excerpted at the beginning of this book.

Additional Implications, or an Extension of the Argument

The argument presented in the previous section has several additional implications for the further development of money markets once they become institutionalized in the manner described above. My argument so far has been consistent with Knight's statement that

> the main goal of those who develop institutional rules is to gain strategic advantage vis-à-vis other actors, and therefore, the substantive content of those rules should generally reflect distributional concerns. The resulting institutions may or may not be socially efficient: It depends on whether or not the institutional form that distributionally favors the actors capable of asserting their strategic advantage is socially efficient. . . . [T]he inefficiency need not arise from any incapacity of the actors . . . but, rather, from their self-interest, their pursuit of a less efficient alternative that gives them a greater individual gain.[23]

A corollary to this is that those advantaged by the institutional status quo have both the incentive and a disproportionate ability to affect the future course of its development, due to the very rules of the institution that they created to their advantage. In this way institutional rules can themselves become additional sources of power asymmetries.

Such a conceptualization of power has no difficulty in accommodating asymmetries of power or bargaining due to institutions. In fact, this framework adds to the explanation for institutional emergence by observing that institutions themselves can become sources of power and accounting for changes in the structure of an already institutionalized money and credit market over time. The specific contents of the credible commitment made to financial capital holders give them an incentive to defend certain basic aspects of the institutional status quo *as financial investors*: that is, as any actor or group that fits this definition. In other words, credible commitments institutionally solidify, or even specify in policy terms, certain interests as those belonging to financiers *as a class.* Therefore investors would oppose policy measures that could potentially lead to significant deviation from certain aspects of the institutional status quo and would have the means, owing to their institutional position, to oppose such measures.[24] However, investors could not be expected to have the same degree of unity on policy issues that would not predictably affect such vital or fundamental features of the institution.

To the extent that investors could not unite over policy preferences beyond the fundamental interests noted above, they would be at a distinct disadvantage vis-à-vis rulers, primarily because they would be highly likely to fail at any endeavor that required collective action. Rulers, on the other hand, due to their institutional position, do not face equivalent challenges in acting collectively.[25] This has important consequences for the regulatory structure of already institutionalized money and credit systems, since established incumbents in the money market would prefer entry to be more, rather than less, restrictive. While individual reasons might be specific to particular policies or contexts, the common underlying feature would be a desire to maintain control by precluding anything that would threaten their established positions, such as destructive competition in the money market.[26]

Turning these preferences into policies, however, requires considerable collective action, particularly in situations where they do not align with the desires of the ruler. Indeed, compared to the conditions that enabled the initial institutionalization—wherein the preferences of all the parties gave them strong incentives to cooperate—the situation would be far more complicated: net gains (to individual investors or financiers) from mutual cooperation would not necessarily exceed those resulting from noncooperation.[27] Depending on the particular scenario, individual investors (or subgroups thereof) might be better off not cooperating or cooperating only if everyone else did. Unlike in the case of basic or fundamental institutional interests, there would not necessarily be any correspondence between the interests of individual investors and the collective interests (if any) of all participants in the money and credit system.[28]

Furthermore, rulers, owing to their institutional position, could propose policy measures designed to have different distributional implications for different subgroups of financial capital holders precisely in order to prevent any collective action; in the process, they could also secure the cooperation of a sufficient subsection of investors to enact those measures. The point here is not that rulers necessarily have preferences that diverge from those of a section of investors. But to the extent that they do have any preferences—for any reason, including ideological ones—that relate to the money and credit system, and these do not threaten the fundamental institutional interests, the difficulty of collective action would vary with the specific (expected) distributional outcomes of those preferences for different (groups of) participants in the money and credit system.[29] Financial capital holders would therefore have an advantage in instances where either policy positions involved fundamental interests or the expected or predicted distributional implications of a policy were such that it was in the interests of investors to cooperate (that is, the alternatives to cooperation were worse). In other words, whatever rulers' preferences over the money market, their realization in policy would be contingent on such policies not disturbing basic institutional pacts and predictably benefiting a large enough constituency of financial capital holders.

Thus one of the *necessary* conditions for regulatory or other changes in the money and credit system is distributional conflicts among financial investors. Rulers could initiate such conflicts as long as their proposed policy did not threaten basic institutional interests and managed to have expected distributional consequences that were sufficient to prevent (oppositional) unity among investors. It follows that incumbents' success in restricting entry into the money market would depend on rulers' preferences and the expected distributional outcomes, for incumbents as well as others, of any changes in entry requirements.

Relating This Extension to Other Arguments: Ideas, Institutions, and Power

The explanation I offer in the previous section for changes within an already institutionalized money and credit system is used to account for some of the major developments in the U.S. financial system during the first third of the nineteenth century. These include the growth of the banking system and the emergence of the first Bank of the United States, the narrow failure of an attempt to renew its federal charter, the establishment of the second Bank of the United States, and finally President Andrew Jackson's vetoing of the bill to renew that Bank's charter, which led indirectly to further growth in the number of state-chartered banks. What follows is an examination of alternative explanations of these developments in light of the framework I proposed in the previous section. While some of these explanations prove inadequate, they can also be adapted to this theoretical framework with some modifications. The following analysis first provides an explication of how the ideology of policy makers fits into the theoretical framework. It then considers the more general question of whether—and to what extent—there is an inherent tension between theoretical accounts that focus on power and distributional considerations, such as this one, and those that stress the importance of ideological motivations in explaining outcomes.

Explanations that emphasize Jackson's ideology or public philosophy—or, more broadly, the role of public philosophies in institutional development and change—tend to neglect the ways in which the interpretation, prominence, and influence of such philosophies are conditional on their expected distributional advantages for relatively powerful individuals and groups.[30] This is not to say that ideologies and public philosophies can be completely reduced to considerations of power and distribution. Rather, my view here borrows from Max Weber's formulation of "elective affinities" among ideas, interests, and objectives of all kinds. According to Weber, "Not ideas, but material and ideal interests, directly govern men's conduct. Yet very frequently the 'world images' that have been created by 'ideas' have, like switchmen, determined the tracks along which action has been pushed by the dynamic of interest."[31] While both abstract interests and more concrete aims such as monetary gain can motivate individuals and provide ends or objectives (for reasons both egotistical and otherwise), ideas about the relationships between means and ends dictate the specific behaviors undertaken to achieve these ends. Individuals therefore prefer ideals or philosophies whose implications most closely approximate the ends they value.[32]

One implication of this view of the relationship between ideas and interests, especially in light of the theoretical framework I present here, is that the effects of these philosophies, whatever their provenance, are mediated by existing institutions and the groups that these institutions empower. A quick examination of an alternative argument about the role of ideology in Jackson's decision to deny the second Bank of the United States a charter renewal illustrates this point.

Susan Hoffmann attributes the demise of the second Bank of the United States largely to Jackson's "individualistic" public philosophy, which saw little role for governments in banking.[33] As she observes, his philosophy held that "there should and could be a clear line between what is public and what is private. The government was public. The economy was private. They should not manipulate each other. Andrew Jackson destroyed the Bank of the United States because it confounded the public and the private in its structure and its purposes."[34] Although this analysis accounts for Jackson's motivation for opposing the Bank, it does not quite succeed in explaining the outcomes, especially the sometimes profound inconsistency between the president's declared views on the issue and what actually transpired. First, agreement with Jackson's philosophy would not necessarily imply opposition to the second Bank, especially given that almost the entire money market—if not the entire economy—of the United States was arguably fundamentally a violation of this principle.[35] As Chapter 5 shows, others sharing Jackson's views on the proper relationship between the government and the economy and his animosity toward banking corporations—including independent artisans and workers' groups, whom Jackson claimed to speak for—nonetheless held the second Bank to be much less objectionable than the numerous state banks that dotted the landscape of the country. Indeed, Jackson's dismissal of William Duane as his treasury secretary was a direct result of this disagreement over the implication of this philosophy for the fate of the second Bank.[36]

Moreover, the second Bank's supporters often drew from the same public philosophy to denounce alternative plans for national banks. A House majority report from 1830 condemned Jackson's plan to replace it with a government bank in these words: "No government . . . of which the committee has any knowledge, except perhaps the despotism of Russia was ever invested with a patronage at once so prodigious in its influence, and so dangerous in its character. In the most desperate financial extremities, no other European government has ventured into an experiment so perilous."[37] This again demonstrates that public philosophies and ideas need not necessarily imply any particular policy positions, let alone outcomes.

Similarly, Hoffmann interprets Jackson's use of "pet banks"—state-chartered banks, so called by opponents because of their perceived closeness to the administration—to transfer government deposits from the second Bank as part of his long-term plan "to gain leverage to curb their [the state banks'] banking practice."[38] Yet to entice them to accept deposits, he told them, "The deposites [*sic*] of the public money will enable you to afford increased facilities to commerce, and to extend your accommodation to individuals."[39] Even assuming that this was a strategic move on his part (though such an assumption would demand some explanation), his efforts at curbing chartered banking and completely severing the link between government and banking seem to have ended in failure, notwithstanding Hoffmann's citation of Jackson's "specie circular" and the subsequent institution of the Independent Treasury, which had a brief run under the Van Buren administration and was reinstated more lastingly in 1846, during George Polk's presidency.[40] The separation of the government from the banking system was carried out only in its breach, since the "treasury's operations continued to influence the money market," the government continued to rely on financiers and bankers for its operations in various ways, and Congress financed the system so poorly that not even the most basic tasks could be carried out without difficulty.[41] Though the Independent Treasury formally continued until 1921, the ostensible principle behind its establishment was explicitly abandoned in the aftermath of the Civil War with the institution of the National Banking System, which created federally chartered banks.

To reiterate, the point here is not that ideas or public philosophies have no role in explanation but that establishing their role without considering the strategic and institutional environment does not provide a complete explanation of the outcomes.[42] Moreover, a focus on philosophies alone leaves open questions such as why certain ideas, or particular interpretations of them, find favor among policy makers or other influential actors. As a corollary, why are others excluded from policy discussions, even though they might be widely accepted among many sectors of the population? Finally, how or why do implications or interpretations of the same public philosophy change over time?[43]

The answer, again, would seem to be one offered earlier—namely, that the reception, interpretation, and enactment of ideas and philosophies are constrained by the dynamics of power and expected distributional consequences. The prominence that ideas attain is related to the power of the agents propounding them; power, in turn, can be explained by prevailing institutional configurations and the position of agents in them. For example, Greta Krippner, in explaining the rise of finance in the U.S. economy since the 1970s, notes the rise of the prescriptive notion that the economy should ideally be "depoliticized."[44] As she further observes, such depoliticization has involved changes in both ideas and institutions, such that "ideational effects rest on what is an *actual* reorganization of material practices."[45] Institutionally privileged actors enacted these changes in reaction to other socially powerful actors and groups.[46] A century and a half earlier, the predecessors of these proponents of depoliticizing the economy made strikingly similar arguments against government ownership or control of banks and too much public input into economic and financial policy. As we shall see, the charters of both the first and the second Banks of the United States were institutional manifestations of this principle. At the same time, both charters also reflected the outcomes of bargains among prominent economic groups. Thus, ideas become prominent when encoded in material (institutional) practices by relatively powerful actors.

On first reading, the view of institutions as outcomes of power asymmetries—exemplified by Knight, among others—may seem to sit uneasily with the relationship between ideas and interests explicated above, especially given Knight's emphasis on instrumental behavior motivated by distributional (or gain-seeking) considerations. Yet some reflection on the relationship between actions and outcomes reveals that distributional (gain-seeking) ends do not necessarily preclude a place for ideas. This is again because a consideration of the best ways to attain given objectives—the relationship between actions and outcomes—perforce implicates ideas. To the extent that an idea about a means-end relationship seems to be the "right" one (i.e., implies the desired outcome), given the available evidence, it fits into a broadly rationalist framework. But if this is not clear, there is still scope for experimentation and learning, just as in the case of uncertainty about institutional outcomes.[47]

A second possible complication in reconciling the status of ideas with the view of institutions as products of power and gain-seeking involves the primacy of self-interested goals in the latter view.[48] However, this need not be a problem for the argument as long as one does not dismiss the possibility that both ideological/nonegoistic and self-interested motivations may operate. Even putatively nonegoistic ideas can have distributional implications for someone motivated by self-interest, even if the original carrier of the idea is not so motivated. Outcomes would then depend on the extent to which these ideas were either deployed effectively or codified in the pursuit of a certain institutional design or policy goal, which would ultimately be contingent on the relative power of social actors pursuing these goals. Thus, as long as it is allowed that power asymmetries can dictate outcomes, this view remains consistent with both kinds of motives operating. For example, in explaining the developments in the U.S. banking system between 1829 and 1836, one could state that although Jackson's ability to undertake certain policy measures depended on the bargaining situation, there was nothing preventing his motivation from being purely ideological (that is, not motivated by egoistic self-interest). At the same time, however, the bargaining situation depended on the distributional implications of the (non-self-interested) measures envisaged for various institutionally advantaged and gain-seeking groups of investors.

Relating This Extension to Other Arguments: The "Investment Theory" and Banking Institutions

As I observed above, the establishment of institutions of credible commitment gives the collective interests of investors a somewhat more concrete form so that the subsequent politics of banking and finance, and hence market development, become explicable in terms of the various policy preferences such institutions engender. The preferences of groups become endogenous to the institutional environment that such credible commitments create, due in part to their distributional implications. This simple insight can clarify and complement other extant explanations that refer to economic interests to explain policy outcomes in the money and credit market of the United States, especially during the first third of the nineteenth century.

Thus, in arguments that implicate economic interests, the demise of the two Banks of the United States is variously attributed to businessmen who sought cheap money (and were frustrated by the two Banks), hard-money agrarians and their ideological allies, or a coalition of the two.[49] None of the works, however, considers the counterfactual question of whether the two Banks would have survived without the intervention of any or all of these groups. This analysis is important if such arguments are to be given a specifically causal interpretation: to say that these factors caused the developments discussed is also to say that the developments would not have taken place without them. In order to empirically demonstrate the plausibility of this counterfactual within a single case, one would have to show that the alternative outcome or development (the one that did not come to pass) was a historical possibility—in that relevant actors recognized it as such—but it did not happen precisely because of the reasons advanced in the theory.[50]

An argument already exists that lends itself to this kind of systematic examination against alternative hypotheses. Thomas Ferguson's "investment theory" argues that due to the costs of entry into the process of political contestation, competition between political parties over economic issues closely reflects the schisms between principal investors in a society. Thus, "on all issues affecting the vital interests that major investors have in common, no party competition will take place."[51] Yet the argument does not comment on why certain interests are recognized as vital while others are not. This presents a slight problem because there are many potential economic issues that are not politically contested, and it becomes difficult to attribute each one of these to either vital (common) investor interests or indifference.[52] The problem is compounded because the theory itself implies that one is unlikely to observe evidence that would allow one to attribute the absence of conflict over a particular topic to the common interest of investors (since such issues may not make an appearance at all). Thus, the evidence for Ferguson's theory mainly comprises affirmative instances of investors splitting on issues and consequent party competition over the same concerns.[53]

Yet his theory seems to be stated as a necessary condition: party competition takes place over issues *only if* investors' interests in them diverge or such issues are irrelevant or marginal to investor interests. It perforce appeals to a counterfactual world where *certain* issues could have been put on the agenda but for the fact that they constituted common vital interests of principal investors. The empirical plausibility of such a scenario would therefore require a demonstration of what these issues were, who championed them, why and how they affected the interests of all investors, and finally how they were excluded from the agenda. All this is eminently achievable with some elaboration of the theory. Instead of assuming that certain interests are vital to investors, the argument could, with little change, be made instead to refer to issues over which investors manage reach a consensus (i.e., they decide that such interests are, indeed, vital). This slight change in emphasis is not merely semantic: any demonstration of the process by which investors identify an issue as important and seek to create consensus over it would constitute evidence in favor of the larger proposition. This, in addition to the demonstration that investors mobilized against policy positions that they perceived as contrary to the common interests they had identified, would represent good evidence in favor of the plausibility of the counterfactual scenario and hence the theory.

This shift in emphasis also allows (institutionally privileged) political actors some agency: it allows for the consideration of hypotheses that see them as sources of investor cohesion and dissension. Thus, instead of focusing on how intra-investor politics influence policy, one can theorize how policy—at times institutionalized or giving rise to new institutions—can dictate the vital interests of major investors.[54] Without altering the central causal mechanism or prediction of Ferguson's investment theory, this reframing permits one to incorporate insights from the literature on institutions in political science and sociology: they are seen as both explananda, or dependent variables, and explanans, or independent variables (insofar as they subsequently affect vital interests). After all, even the most obvious of interests, seemingly requiring no further explanation—namely, profit—assumes the existence of a market, which is an institution.[55]

Making these changes to the phrasing of the theory does have the potential, however, to indicate a different interpretation of events. Thus, for instance, in briefly considering the relevance of the investment theory for the politics of the Jacksonian period, Ferguson mainly relies on the work of Bray Hammond in arguing that the forces resisting the second Bank comprised "many state bankers, who did not conceal their desire to smash the Bank."[56] Showing the opposition of a few bankers to the second Bank cannot be sufficient evidence for the investment theory, since it does not address the appropriate counterfactual scenario. It could easily be claimed that the Bank would have collapsed even without the participation of these anti-Bank bankers. In other words, it remains to be demonstrated that dissension among the ranks of bankers was *necessary* for the collapse of the Bank.[57] As I demonstrate in Chapter 5, dissension among bankers was, indeed, necessary for the collapse of the second Bank; yet the evidence for this is not the initial opposition of some state bankers to the Bank. The supporters of the Bank had succeeded in achieving sufficient consensus among investors to renew the charter.[58] Indeed, this remained highly probable even after Jackson's veto. It was an act of the executive—*after* the presidential veto of the charter—that fractured that consensus and thus definitively destroyed the Bank.

The Cases and the Method

The theoretical statements here and throughout the book imply the possibilities of different worlds: they insist that if certain conditions had been different, history would have unfolded somewhat differently. Yet these different worlds—the different possible ways of history unfolding—were not realized precisely because those certain conditions were, in fact, *not* different. For this reason these statements are called contrary-to-fact conditionals, or counterfactuals. The importance of such statements in the social sciences, including political science, is well recognized. As Jack Levy points out in the *Oxford Handbook of Political Methodology*, "All causal statements imply some kind of counterfactual. A historical argument that a particular set of conditions, processes, and events caused, influenced, or contributed to a subsequent set of conditions, processes, and events implies that if the antecedent conditions had been different, the outcome would have been different."[59] The task of empirical investigation would be to evaluate the plausibility of such counterfactual statements, in this case purely observationally. What kind of (observational) evidence, in other words, would be relevant to plausibly demonstrating that the world envisaged by a counterfactual statement would have been realized had the antecedent conditions been as the statement specifies?[60] To simplify quite a bit, in historical research in the social sciences the usual method of substantiating counterfactual statements is to define cases by time intervals containing the variation in outcomes that the theory predicts and compare them over two or more such intervals (with different outcomes) in order to examine whether a change in the key factors the theory has identified does, indeed, result in something approximating the counterfactual outcome(s). Alternatively, researchers define and compare cases across space to see whether a variation in explanatory factors across (broadly similar or different) cases results in approximations of the relevant counterfactuals.[61] The discussion below addresses how counterfactuals are substantiated in this argument, not just by comparing cases over time and across space but also by considering the (observable) possibility of the counterfactual outcome—the outcome that did not actually happen—within the same case (that is, without the aid of comparison cases, where something akin to the counterfactual outcome might have occurred).

Because my argument concerns the emergence and legacies of the financial institutions it discusses, tracing their historical development becomes imperative. The cases examined in this project are those of India and the United States, which I chose in order to illuminate the reasons for the lack of the emergence of indigenous, institutionalized money and credit systems. These two cases are especially instructive, since they represent prototypically divergent trajectories in the development of nineteenth-century public credit and money markets. Though not necessarily completely independent of one another, they are contemporaneous and thus more useful than cases widely separated in time. My project requires contemporaneous cases for precisely the same reasons that it necessitates the tracing of historical trajectories: the initial form of the money and credit system would have affected subsequent developments, causing cases separated in time to diverge so much as to render them unsuitable for such comparisons.

I compare the two cases across space while also comparing each to country to itself at different times. The argument follows the case of the United States from the 1750s—when there were no formal, organized markets or financial institutions—to the establishment of the first banks in the aftermath of the Revolutionary War, and then from the emergence of state-backed money and credit systems to the second Bank of the United States' loss of the federal charter.[62] I then trace the case of India from the precolonial period to the establishment of the East India Company state and then its formal acquisition by the British Crown. Such a comparison serves to demonstrate that the same factors—including the motivations of key actors, as identified in the theoretical argument—can explain the lack of an institutionalized public credit and money market in two otherwise vastly different contexts.[63] It also demonstrates that the relevant factors changed over time in only one of the cases, producing the phenomena central to this book: the divergent trajectories in institutional development.

It could still be argued, even allowing for the relevance of the cited factors, that the United States is not the most plausible counterfactual (or contrast) to the Indian case.[64] This is because, first, unlike in the longitudinal case in the United States, the relevant causal factors do not change in the way (longitudinally) that would have produced the United States–like outcome in India. This allows for the possibility that there are other, more relatively plausible contrasts; or that something else other than an outcome similar to that in the United Sates would have occurred, had the relevant causal factors been different. To state the same point more generally, let "A" and "X" be the two suggested contrasting outcomes, such that part of what it is to be "X" is that it is "not-A," and part of what it is to be "A" is that it is "not-X." That "A" and "X" are really contrasts of one another can be empirically demonstrated by defining and comparing cases across space to see whether a variation in explanatory factors across cases results in approximations of the relevant counterfactuals: that is, whether a variation in the identified explanatory factors does indeed produce either "X" or "A." Both "X" and "A" are outcomes in the (longitudinal) case of the United States, but only "X" takes place in the case of India. The criticism, therefore, is that one could not rule out the possibility of any number of alternative possible worlds or outcomes other than "A," all of which would fit the definition of "not-X" (say, B C, D . . .) in the case of India, especially if even the *possibility* of "A" is unobservable. Thus, the case of India could be deemed at least irrelevant to the theoretical framework.

Yet if it were to be demonstrated that the particular counterfactual world envisaged by the theory (the world "A") was, indeed, an observable possibility in the case of India, and was not realized for precisely the reasons the theory specifies, this would increase the plausibility of the counterfactual. This demonstration could be achieved by showing that relevant actors or groups were aware of the counterfactual possibilities ("A") envisaged in the theory, but rejected them precisely for the reasons anticipated by the theory.[65] This, in other words, would establish "A" as the most plausible contrasting outcome to "X," given the antecedent conditions specified in the theory. This work relies on this device to establish the plausibility of alternative possible worlds, while at the same time demonstrating that such worlds failed to materialize for the reasons specified in the theoretical framework.

In the case of India (Chapter 4), a historical accident during the establishment of the East India Company (henceforth EIC, or the Company) state allows one to consider the counterfactual possibility that an integrated (i.e., including indigenous bankers and merchants), state-supported financial system *could have* emerged—and relevant actors were aware of such a possibility—if not for the absence of certain crucial factors underlined in the theoretical argument, namely, those that could have enhanced the bargaining power of indigenous investors. Similarly, in empirically substantiating the extension of the framework in the context of an already institutionalized system in the United States, this book considers alternative policy proposals that did not succeed because the necessary conditions stated in the argument were absent. Thus, Chapter 5 demonstrates that policy proposals that contradicted the collective preferences of all investors—such as Jackson's plan for a bank founded entirely on the credit of the federal government, or even before that, Albert Gallatin's proposal to alter the charter of the first Bank of the United States—failed to reach any kind of policy agenda, just as would be expected in an explanation based on the theoretical framework.

To summarize, the explanation takes counterfactual possibilities seriously, not just as theoretical devices but also as empirical possibilities. Thus, in explaining "why A, rather than X," one must demonstrate that both A and X were possibilities according to the empirical conditions at the time and, moreover, relevant actors recognized them as such, but only one was theoretically probable. The contrast case (i.e., the outcome other than the one that actually occurred) must be possible but theoretically improbable: it could have occurred, but failed to do so—precisely because of the reasons advanced by the theory or argument in question. To take the example of India again, Chapter 4 substantiates the counterfactual that a modern banking system could have emerged, had the bargaining situation between indigenous financiers and the EIC been different, by (empirically) demonstrating that the alternative outcome (i.e., the one that failed to occur) was a real historical possibility that policy makers recognized but that failed to materialize because of the Company's bargaining advantage.

Public Credit and the Emergence
of a Money and Credit System
in the United States

A S RICHARD SYLLA POINTS OUT, "As late as 1780, there were no American coins (in the narrow, U.S., sense of America; coins from Spanish America were in common use), no commercial banks, [and] no organized securities markets, and there were few business corporations operating in the country."[1] However, between 1782 and 1791, there were 3 banks in operation, and by 1800 the number of banks had increased to 29. This number had reached 90 by 1811, and almost 250 by 1817.[2] How and why did this happen? And why did such markets not develop before 1780?

The answers to these questions are intertwined. In order to understand the emergence of a money and credit market in the postrevolutionary United States, it is important to examine the financial relations between what were then the British colonies of North America and the British Crown. This section therefore seeks to explain the absence of a commercial banking system and an institutionalized debt market in the colonies. Specifically, it links this to the financial relationship existing between the colonies and the mother country prior to the revolution. Demand for a money market was absent from both the governing authorities and the colonial merchants, and this lack could be traced directly to the structure of the relationships between the Crown and British creditors and between these creditors and colonial merchants. This tripartite structure—the great asymmetry in power between colonial merchants and the British creditors backed institutionally by the Crown—was an example of the kind of colonial relationship that was deleterious to the emergence of institutionalized indigenous or local money and credit markets.

A fundamental fact about the trade relations between the North American colonies and Great Britain was that the colonies generally had a trade deficit with the mother country.[3] One consequence of this was that the colonies were chronically short of hard money, or specie, since any available specie was invariably shipped to Britain to pay for manufacturing goods.[4] As a result, colonial merchants (that is, merchants based in the colonies) had to rely on sterling credits from British traders to make up the difference. Thus, their profits depended to a great extent on British credit. For the purposes of domestic trade and commerce, merchants first "developed an extensive system of book credit and barter. . . . [P]rivate credit instruments such as promissory notes or notes of hand, while they did not generally circulate except within the mercantile community, also enjoyed wide use from the beginning."[5] These early notes were limited, and proposals for more extensive circulation of merchants' notes, backed by property, were often declared illegal.[6] Indeed, the British government generally forbade legal tender notes, fixed the exchange value of the dollar, and closed down colonial mints.[7] British authorities tolerated bills of credit issued by colonial assemblies and the so-called "land banks" or "loan offices" only for the purposes of supporting the numerous wars for control of North America.[8] To gain British approval, these measures had to be temporary: provision had to be made for the retirement of bills and notes by taxation. Moreover, such bills and notes were only rarely accepted as legal tender in payments to British merchants.[9] In other words, to the extent that "private . . . promissory notes" and similar instruments circulated, they were often informal in the sense that they were not backed by the state and hence were denied official status.

It is not difficult to understand why the British government would look askance at banks and other credit institutions in the colonies or why it generally favored an anti-inflationary policy and insisted as a matter of principle on hard-money payments (thus disfavoring paper currency), especially in transactions involving payments outside the colonies. After all, the British government—as far as financial policies toward the colonies were concerned—was most responsive to British merchant-creditors. These creditors, in turn, would generally be unlikely to acquiesce to policies that could devalue the debts owed to them. In fact, one would expect them to oppose any policy that could allow colonists independent control over currency. On the other hand, the failure of colonial merchants to agitate for credit and other financial institutions presents more of a puzzle. To understand it, we need to examine the tripartite relationship between colonial merchants, their British creditors, and the Board of Trade in London, which was the primary body responsible for formulating economic policies for the colonies.

The Board of Trade advised the Privy Council on matters of trade and finance, while the Council instructed the governors of various colonies to either approve or disallow acts passed in the assemblies. Though the Board formally represented the imperial government, in practice it represented the interests of British creditors. Policy debates within the Board—particularly about the wisdom of allowing colonial assemblies to temporarily issue currencies—generally mirrored disagreements among British merchant-creditors. These creditors were not categorically opposed to temporary issuances of currency: a blanket opposition to any paper currency, especially in light of the acute scarcity of specie, would have also hurt them.[10] Disagreements stemmed from the fact that individual creditors faced different levels of risk from the default or diminution of debts. Risks varied based on portfolio, colony, and past experience, especially the behavior of colonial assemblies with regard to the issuing of temporary currency.

Though issuances of notes were ostensibly temporary, many colonial legislatures had a tendency to extend their terms by recirculating the notes or failing to levy adequate taxes; as a result, "large sums [would become] outstanding at one time."[11] The Board of Trade was not the only body that strongly disapproved of such actions: colonial merchants often joined them in this sentiment. Though they were debtors to British merchants, colonial merchants were generally creditors to farmers and planters. Therefore, *within* the colonies, merchants would have wanted control over decisions about the issuance of credit notes. To the extent that actors other than merchant-creditors were in charge of such decisions, there was always the danger that merchant debts—any debts, for that matter—would be devalued by excessive issuances from those who stood to gain from such devaluation. Furthermore, such devaluation also had the potential to adversely affect colonial merchants' relationships with their own creditors.

Since note issuances were voted on by provincial assemblies, control over these events would require significant—perhaps a majority—representation in such assemblies. However, if merchants did not have sufficient representation in the assemblies, they could also join British creditors and the Board of Trade in opposing the issuances. Thus, where there was a convergence in the preferences of British and colonial merchants, and where the latter had sufficient representation in the legislatures, British creditors were more likely to be tolerant of short-term issuances.[12] Policies determined by the Board of Trade, however, applied to all the colonies. There were always occasions on which, owing to the differing extents of merchant control over the assemblies, colonial reactions to the Board's decisions varied. Depending on the circumstances and their position, merchants could either petition the Board of Trade through their British counterparts and trading partners to oppose additional or excessive issuances by assemblies or join fellow colonists in protesting British prohibitions against issuances in general. Additionally, and notwithstanding the relative tolerance of (British) creditors toward issuances from merchant-controlled assemblies, on occasions when the two groups disagreed on what constituted "excessive," colonial merchants could generally come to some kind of an agreement with their British creditors, since both sides had incentives to do so.

In provinces where the merchants had some control over issuances, such as New York and Pennsylvania, they had little incentive to disrupt the status quo in favor of forming commercial banks, since British credit normally sufficed. When colonial merchants did not have control over issuances, they often opposed them, thus finding themselves in a position similar to that of the Board of Trade and British merchants. We can now summarize the logic behind the lack of demand for banks on the part of colonial merchants.

Insofar as colonial merchants depended on British credit for their business, they were loath to jeopardize their only source of long-term credit by strongly favoring paper currency against the wishes of their creditors. The second reason was that since they were creditors themselves and lacked control over assemblies, they feared the diminution of debts owed to them. Establishing commercial banks would have allowed them to control their own credit, particularly at times when their preferences were at odds with that of their British creditors. But this too would have required some control over the assemblies. Without this control, they could not expect to establish a bank on their terms or dictate the issuance of notes, but they could try to prevent excessive issuance by appealing to the Board of Trade, where they were certain to find allies. Thus, while lack of control over assemblies prevented the formation of commercial banks in some cases, control over assemblies obviated such banks in others: control over currency issuances, coupled with the expectation of continuing British credit, was, in fact, a better substitute.

The preceding discussion explains the variation in support, on the part of colonial merchants, for the various acts that the British parliament passed in an effort to control money and credit in the North American colonies. For example, many Massachusetts and Rhode Island merchants actually supported the Currency Act of 1751, which prohibited the governors, councils, or assemblies of the New England colonies from assenting to any new issuances of bills of credit except during emergencies; if such bills were issued, provision had to be made for their retirement (by establishing a tax fund, for example) within a period of five years. The act also stipulated that bills of credit could not be a legal tender in private transactions.[13] Conversely, attempts at currency restriction proved extremely unpopular among merchants in Pennsylvania, New York, and New Jersey.[14] In fact, when the Currency Act of 1764 sought to apply similar restrictions to all the colonies, merchants from the middle colonies led the repeal effort.[15] As Leslie Brock describes, even as the merchants of Rhode Island were petitioning the king about excessive currency issuances around 1749, the leaders of Pennsylvania and New York were mobilizing their English merchant allies, who "could always be relied upon to say a good word for the paper currency of the province[s]."[16] In both instances, the eventual outcomes also depended on the orientation of British merchant-creditors. The fact that many British merchants were more willing to tolerate limited paper issuances in Pennsylvania and New York than in Massachusetts, Rhode Island, or South Carolina accounts for the eventual, though imperfect and late, success of the colonial merchants from the two middle colonies.[17]

An examination of the composition of the respective assemblies demonstrates that, consistent with my argument, merchants opposed the issuance of notes and supported the policies of the Crown precisely in colonies where they had little to no representation in legislative assemblies. Conversely, merchants opposed restrictions in colonies where they all but controlled the respective colonial legislative assemblies. Though systematic and complete data on the membership of all the pertinent colonial assemblies, especially the members' socioeconomic backgrounds and individual political positions, does not seem to exist, some historical studies in combination with data about the memberships of some of the middle and northern assemblies permit relevant inferences.[18]

To contemporaneous observers of colonial politics, Massachusetts seemed to be the most "democratic" colony, and its assembly was said to live up to this reputation.[19] A law that "greatly favored the small agricultural towns over the larger seacoast towns" governed the apportionment of representatives.[20] Merchants, who were concentrated in the coastal cities, were as a result likely to be at a disadvantage as far as representation was concerned. The six major seaports—likely to contain the largest concentration of merchants—could send at most 14 representatives in total to the assembly of potentially 350 members.[21] Even if we consider the entire eastern shore of Massachusetts, the number of members sent to the assembly from this region between 1740 and 1755 represented less than a quarter of the total membership during this time interval.[22] Representatives from the principal seaports, however, did hold a disproportionate share of the assembly's committee assignments. Half of all committee positions in this period were held by just under half of the seaport representatives; Boston alone was responsible for 28 percent of the assignment holders.[23]

It cannot be assumed, however, that every representative from Boston or other major seaports was a merchant or represented merchant interests, as the observations of prominent merchant assembly members such as Thomas Hutchinson (future governor, the speaker of the assembly in the late 1740s, and a foe of paper money) indicate. After losing the election of 1749 for supporting hard-money policies, Hutchinson wrote that he "could but make about 200 votes in near 700 . . . [and] they were the principal [conceivably the most prominent, which would normally tend to correlate with wealth] inhabitants," adding that this obviously was not enough, since "we are governed not by weight but by numbers."[24] Similar statements from Massachusetts governor William Shirley and John Adams, though far from conclusive, at least point to the possibility that not all representatives from the seaport towns were merchants or represented the interests of the mercantile community.[25] In fact, this could be the reason for R. M. Zemsky's observation that "a House leader [a person having a disproportionate share of all committee assignments] was almost as likely to support inflation and deficit financing as he was to endorse hard money and balanced budgets."[26]

That the majority of the Massachusetts assembly (perhaps more than 65 percent) supported frequent currency emissions during the 1740s is well documented, but the point of the evidence above was to trace this to the relative weakness of merchants in the assembly.[27] Nonetheless, when price inflation of basic commodities such as wheat and molasses accompanied excessive depreciation, opponents of paper currency, aided by two large parliamentary grants as payment for Massachusetts's participation in King George's War, managed—in their second try and by an extremely narrow margin—to pass legislation banning paper currency and transitioning to specie.[28] This legislation essentially appropriated the ability of the assembly to issue paper currency; consequently, all future excessive financial expenses would have to be met by borrowing. This meant that representation in the assembly, or lack thereof, would henceforth be irrelevant to ensuring lender representation in matters of financial policy. The Massachusetts act had little effect on the issuance of bills of credit and currency notes by other New England assemblies, especially Rhode Island. Since bills from neighboring provinces circulated freely in Massachusetts and efforts at curbing their circulation met with only modest success, Massachusetts and Rhode Island merchants' support for the 1751 act was not surprising.[29]

In contrast to the Massachusetts case, merchants in both New York and Pennsylvania had ample representation in state assemblies in the decades leading up to the Currency Act of 1764. In the New York assembly, at various points, prominent merchants led both the "court party" and the "popular party," which were the two most prominent rival political factions.[30] According to some historians, the basis of these two factions was more cultural and religious than political and economic.[31] In fact, the founders of the "popular" Whig Party, also known as "independent" or "anti-Crown," were generally from the same milieu as their "court party" opponents, or Tories. William Livingston was only the most prominent example of this phenomenon.[32] As Charles Levermore writes:

> Livingston and his friends were aristocratic Whigs, equally anxious to clip the pinions of ambitious royalty and to curb the insolence of the unlettered mob. The Livingston party of New York did . . . cherish . . . the doctrine that "all authority is derived from the people," but they were quite content with the narrow English definition of the term "people." . . . [T]hey thought that a parliamentary assembly of aristocratic representatives of the people was an ideally perfect form of government.[33]

What distinguished the Whigs from the Tories, led by the DeLanceys, was their lack of deference to the British Crown and their insistence on formulating policy independent of its wishes. It is therefore not surprising that when it came to certain specific economic questions, both the DeLancey and the Livingston factions often opposed Lieutenant Governor Cadwallader Colden.[34]

Currency emissions from New York generally conform to the expectations one would have of an assembly where merchants had strong representation and control. In fact, as Richard Lester has noted, the middle colonies, including New York, "were . . . rather conservative in their use of currency issues."[35] Brock adds, "There appears never to have been a large debtor element bent upon depreciation for depreciation's sake."[36] In addition, there is not much evidence that the currency issuance was the basis of a major political rift between the parties before the passage of the Currency Act of 1764, especially when compared to Massachusetts, where this was an important electoral concern.

As in New York, merchants in the Pennsylvania assembly had substantial and highly conspicuous representation in the two principal political factions, the Quaker Party and the Proprietary Party. Furthermore, there is some evidence that religious distinctions were more salient in the Quaker-Proprietary distinction than any fundamental disagreement on economic issues, particularly monetary concerns. Thus, during the early part of the eighteenth century, opposition to the Quaker Party consisted largely of Anglicans, while later Presbyterians became "the chief antagonists of the Quaker party and the backbone of the Proprietary party."[37] This, in turn, was related to another important issue, again ostensibly linked to religious beliefs: the strong aversion of the Quakers to the various colonial wars.[38]

The two most famous and notable members of the Proprietary group—Thomas Willing and his associate Robert Morris, who would become crucial participants in the revolution and the construction of the new financial system—were also two of the most prosperous merchants not only of Pennsylvania but of the colonies as a whole.[39] The Quaker Party, led by Benjamin Franklin (who was not a member of the Quaker religion) after 1751, also consisted of prominent merchants, such as Joseph Galloway and Samuel Wharton; it dominated the assembly until 1764.[40] It was not until the Stamp Act of 1765 that the Quakers lost control of the assembly, when the Proprietary merchant politicians took advantage of them "[blundering] into a position of appearing to support the [stamp] act."[41]

Although there is plenty of evidence of other, similar divisions, few indications exist that the two parties differed fundamentally on monetary policy, although some merchants of the Proprietary Party did object to the currency emissions of 1723.[42] British merchants trading in Pennsylvania generally approved of the "modest" issuances, and contemporary historians have observed that the paper circulation was "gradual yet moderate."[43]

To summarize, credit relations between the colonies and the metropole constituted an impediment to the formation of colonial commercial banks. Colonial merchants generally relied on their British counterparts for credit. The availability of credit, in turn, was contingent on a host of political and economic factors in the metropolis, not all under the control of the colonial merchants. The one thing the merchants could potentially control was the temporary emission of bills of credit or currency (through land banks, for instance), precisely to deal with such eventualities as temporary credit scarcity. But this was crucially contingent on their having sufficient representation in colonial assemblies. When they did not have such control, currency issuances directly threatened their own interests, so the only options left to them were to appeal to the Board of Trade to stop emissions or support its efforts to prevent them. When they did have sufficient control, they could generally convince their creditors and the Board of Trade to allow limited currency emissions, which again obviated credit institutions in the colonies. The structure of the situation—owing to the differences in bargaining power between colonial merchants, on one hand, and the Crown and British creditors on the other—was such that it restricted the possible courses of action of colonial merchants: in Knight's words, one group was able, due to this situation, to "to affect by some means the alternatives available to . . . [another] person or group."[44]

The incentives of the colonial merchants could be expected to change if either the assemblies controlled by merchants were permanently prevented from issuing any currency or merchants had reasons to believe that British credit would not be forthcoming in the future. In case only the currency ban happened, the first preference of the merchants would have been the restoration of the original status quo. This preference, however, would have depended on how the costs, benefits, and probabilities of such an endeavor compared to those of establishing new commercial banks. Assuming that the benefits would have been the same in either case, the costs of creating commercial banks and the chances of their success would have appeared to exceed the costs of petitioning the Board of Trade for a repeal of the ban and the probability that such petitions would succeed because, as noted earlier, colonial merchants had British allies who were willing to speak on their behalf. Even the failure of petition efforts would not necessarily have led to the formation of banks if British creditors had been willing to make up for the loss of the ability to issue currency by proportionately augmenting the amount of credit granted. Only if the second event alone took place (merchants believed that British credit would not be forthcoming in the future), or if both events happened simultaneously, would it have been necessary for commercial banks to emerge to substitute for the loss of external credit. Because Britain had been the sole source of colonial credit for over a hundred years, only a sociopolitical event of some magnitude could have succeeded in permanently modifying the expectations and hence the preferences of the colonial merchants. The American Revolution proved to be such an event.

EMERGENCE OF A FINANCIAL SYSTEM

British actions after the Treaty of Paris in 1763 disturbed the hitherto prevalent state of affairs. The Currency Act of 1764, the Stamp Act of 1765, the Townshend Acts, and finally the Act of 1773 (which, among other things, allowed the East India Company to sell directly to retailers, thus eliminating the colonial merchant completely from transactions) progressively increased the costs of trade for colonial merchants. These merchants had hitherto functioned under the aegis of British imperial rule, which had certain advantages, although the metropole was not directly responsive to their concerns. To a large extent, their very position in the imperial trading system was predicated on British rules and regulations. While these laws were not of their creation and remained beyond their direct control, colonial merchants had adapted to them in ways that enabled them to function profitably within the larger British trading empire. Most colonial merchants were both importers and exporters, and Britain was the chief destination for both kinds of shipment.[45] Merchants reacted to these acts by seeking to overturn them, but on every occasion the Crown failed to restore the previous status quo.[46] At the same time, the oppositional movement produced a group of potential governing elites comprising merchants in the northern and middle colonies and southern planters who championed political autonomy for the colonists.[47] By the early 1770s, this movement had emerged as a viable (from the merchants' perspective) alternative to British governance.[48]

As this section demonstrates, sufficient merchant support was crucial if this movement were to succeed. On the other hand, British intransigence substantially increased the costs of the status quo for many merchants. In other words, while the new group's only source of immediate finance was the domestic merchants, the merchants' alternatives were also highly circumscribed. The potential new source of political authority held out the promise of not only the amelioration of long-standing economic complaints but also the opening up of economic opportunities that had not existed before the colonial disturbances began. This state of affairs provided the impetus for the first banks in the United States. However, the process was neither automatic nor smooth. It took some of the new political elite some time to perceive their dependence on merchants and take steps that would make the outcomes that the merchants desired seem more likely. As a result, some time elapsed before merchants perceived the emergence of a viable *economic* alternative to British rule as a highly probable event. It was this shift in perspective that triggered the exchange leading to the formation of banks. I do not seek to explain the American Revolution here: while the reasons why subsets of merchants may or may not have supported the revolution are important to this chapter, its causes as a whole are irrelevant to this framework. In other words, the revolution can be considered either exogenous or endogenous to the explanation, and its exogeneity or endogeneity does not affect the logic of the foregoing explanation.

Mutual Dependence

The events and political activities that escalated with the Declaration of Independence confronted North American governing elites with the necessity of mobilizing resources to defend their newly declared sovereignty as well as the government's internal hierarchy. Significant financial resources would be required to wage war and also to ensure the authoritative implementation of domestic decisions. For example, they would need to pay, clothe, arm, feed, medically attend to, and provide shelter for soldiers, as well as maintain internal order, punish criminals, prevent hoarding of essential commodities, prevent black-marketeering, prevent commerce with the British, and generally prevent and punish any activities determined to be treasonous. In addition to the financial resources required to carry out these activities, rulers also needed resources in the very short term. What, then, were their options? Rulers' possible (and mutually nonexclusive) sources of income can be listed as follows:

1. Rent from land and other property taxes: this would have involved taxing landholders both large and small (e.g., planters and independent farmers). This would almost certainly have also led to taxing those renting from large landholders, since these property owners would have passed on some of the tax to their renters
2. Sale of land, including land acquired through the various wars and treaties in the past as well as land seized
3. External borrowing (i.e., borrowing from foreign governments or markets)
4. Domestic borrowing (i.e., borrowing from domestic capital holders)

These options, apart from the first to a certain degree, would have required extensive cooperation from merchant capital holders. The sale of land would have necessitated the availability of buyers with the ability to pay the sums required, preferably in hard money. Only merchants had sufficient wealth to be able to do this. Similarly, only merchants had contacts with financiers in overseas capital markets, so their cooperation would have been integral to any effort at borrowing funds from abroad. Finally, merchants were the only group that collectively held enough capital to lend to the government. While the scale of resources available from land rent (option 1) might seem large enough to compensate for the other three sources, there were multiple reasons that this was an untenable solution.

Exclusive, even disproportionate, reliance on land rents in the short term would have entailed a dramatic and immediate increase in the level of taxes. This, in turn, would have alienated most of the population—particularly the very sectors that provided troops and other logistical support for the revolution. The provincial governments had traditionally levied land and other property taxes to finance the various colonial wars. But even with periodic taxes in certain provinces that were relatively high by world standards, and contributions from the Crown, most provincial governments failed to retire wartime currency issuances. The total cost to the colonies of the Seven Years' War came to about £2,568,248 (sterling), of which £1,068,769 (41.6 percent) was reimbursed by the British parliament.[49] Even with this subsidy, taxation levels in provinces such as Massachusetts and South Carolina between 1758 and 1760 were quite high by world standards, and by 1763, only about 70 percent of the total debt had been repaid.[50] As a point of comparison, the new Continental government had already issued $25,000,000 in notes in 1776 alone, excluding the notes that various provincial governments had issued.[51] The exact determination of the value of this new currency vis-à-vis British pounds sterling is difficult, but Robert Morris is recorded as noting to the Commissioners in Paris, in the latter half of 1776, that most people were refusing to accept the new currency and that "£250 continental money, or 666⅔ dollars, is given for a bill of exchange of £100 sterling."[52] Assuming the accuracy of Morris's estimate, this would imply a sterling debt of approximately £3,500,000 in just one year, more than the total cost of the Seven Years' War, due only to Continental Congress currency emissions. Indeed, this is probably an underestimation of the actual cost: according to Anne Bezanson, Morris might well have been exaggerating the depreciation of dollar bills relative to the pound.[53]

While the new Continental Congress did not have any taxation powers or capacities, the states could, in theory, have levied taxes. However, as E. James Ferguson points out, "The state governments were embryonic and sometimes wracked by internal commotion. Their legality was not firmly established, and they were more disposed to court a popular following than levy rigorous taxes which would suggest an onerous comparison with the enemy."[54] Neither the scale of revenue available nor the costs of acquiring this revenue justified reliance on land taxes. Rulers were consequently left with options 2, 3, and 4, all of which required cooperation from capital holders.

Merchants who had hitherto either supported or generally adhered to nonimportation and the other agitations right up to the first Continental Association faced the following set of choices with the outbreak of hostilities in Lexington and Concord. They could:

1. Declare support for the patriots and hence independence
2. Declare opposition to political independence
3. Declare their neutrality

To address the net benefits merchants would have perceived in options 1 and 2, it would be reasonable to discount the role of their predictions regarding the eventual outcome of the revolution in their calculations because of (a) the high degree of uncertainty and (b) the effects of their own support on the outcome of the revolution. Any prediction of the future would have been contingent on a number of factors, none of which were stable or could be ascertained with any degree of accuracy. For example, one factor determining success was the extent of the support that the new governing elites could garner from Britain's imperial rivals. Thus, there were ongoing efforts to elicit French support for the colonial cause. French support, in turn, was influenced by a host of factors, most of which were not under the colonists' control and very few of which were either known or predictable on the part of the colonial governing elites.[55] A second factor would have been the ability of the newly constituted elites to mount an effective military effort. But this possibility, as should be evident from the discussion in the previous section, was itself contingent on merchant support. For all merchants knew, then, revolutionary success was partly dependent on their collective support. This, in turn, would have reduced merchants' calculations to the costs and benefits of eventual independence, disregarding the kind of probabilities (e.g., the probability of success) that normally go into calculations of utility. What, then, were these expected costs and benefits?

The major benefits of being a part of the imperial trading system were noted in the first section of this chapter. But the expected costs and benefits of each option were not uniformly distributed among all merchants. At the aggregate level, limiting the discussion to commercial relations for the moment, the expected net cost of independence would have been much higher for southern merchants than northern merchants; conversely, southerners' net benefits were likely to be lower. This is because southern merchants were, relatively speaking, greater beneficiaries of British trade than their northern counterparts

(Tables 3.1 and 3.2). While southern merchants were restricted to the British market as a source of their imports and destination for their exports, northern merchants carried out substantial trade (both legal and illicit) with southern Europe and the West Indies. Moreover, even in their British trade, northern merchants generally employed their own vessels at a rate far higher than their southern counterparts did—to such an extent, in fact, that they became a threat to Britain-based merchants.[56]

Among northern merchants, there would have been further variation depending on the composition of their trade portfolios. Expected net costs would be much smaller to merchants whose portfolios comprised mostly trade with continental Europe, with the non-British West Indies, or with colonies in North America than to those that traded mostly with Britain. Similarly, the expected costs to merchants who indulged in smuggling were likely to be much smaller, since the various acts beginning with the First Act of 1764 had progressively made smuggling very difficult. In addition to differences in trading portfolios, the expectation of land acquisition would also have made independence more lucrative for some merchants than others. Merchants who wished to speculate on western lands but were held back by British laws would have welcomed political independence under the expectation that it would open up speculation opportunities.

TABLE 3.1. THE SHARE OF EACH COLONIAL REGION'S COMMODITY EXPORTS TO EACH OVERSEAS AREA AND (IN PARENTHESES) REGIONAL SHARES OF TOTAL EXPORTS TO EACH AREA, 1768–1772

	Great Britain and Ireland	Southern Europe	West Indies	Africa
New England	18 (5)	14 (12)	64 (39)	4 (93)
Middle Colonies	23 (8)	33 (34)	44 (32)	0 (5)
Upper South	83 (57)	9 (19)	8 (13)	0 (0)
Lower South	88 (26)	0 (10)	12 (14)	0 (2)

Source: J. F. Shepherd and G. M. Walton, "Trade, Distribution, and Economic Growth in Colonial America," *Journal of Economic History* 32, no. 1 (1972): 134, 136.

Note: Because other regions are not included in shares of total exports, percentages do not always equal 100.

TABLE 3.2 THE SHARE OF EACH REGION'S COMMODITY IMPORTS FROM EACH OVERSEAS AREA AND (IN PARENTHESES) REGIONAL SHARES OF TOTAL IMPORTS FROM EACH AREA, 1768–1772

	Great Britain and Ireland	Southern Europe	West Indies	Africa
New England	66 (20)	2 (23)	32 (43)	0
Middle Colonies	76 (26)	3 (42)	21 (32)	0
Upper South	89 (29)	1 (14)	10 (14)	0
Lower South	86 (13)	1 (9)	13 (9)	0

Source: J. F. Shepherd and G. M. Walton, "Trade, Distribution, and Economic Growth in Colonial America," *Journal of Economic History* 32, no. 1 (1972): 135, 136.

Note: Because other regions are not included in shares of total imports, percentages do not always equal 100.

That most of the considerations discussed above were operative is shown by a letter originally published in Philadelphia in 1776 and addressed to partisans on both sides of the independence question. The address asks merchants to carefully consider the same costs and benefits of independence discussed in the previous paragraph.[57] There were, additionally, attempts at convincing wavering merchants that their interests lay with political independence. The most famous of these, Thomas Paine's "Common Sense," noted that "America would have flourished as much, and probably much more, had no European power taken any notice of her. The commerce by which she hath enriched herself are the necessities of life, and will always have a market while eating is the custom of Europe."[58] Others averred that the benefits of independence included "a free and unlimited trade; a great accession of wealth, and a proportionable rise in the value of land; the establishment, gradual improvement, and perfection of manufactures and science; a vast influx of foreigners . . . [and] an astonishing increase of our people from present stock."[59] Additionally, merchants were repeatedly assured, in words and in deeds, that their property would be given even better protection than the British had provided. The articles and pamphlets that promised vast economic improvements also promised that America would be a country "where encouragement is given to industry; where liberty and property are well secured."[60] And despite some property damage during the Stamp Act riots, the incipient political authority—especially its moderate wing—always ensured that protests did not result in the seizure and destruction of merchant property and generally looked askance at mob actions that had the potential to indiscriminately cause property damage.[61]

As for option 3, merchants whose portfolios were more or less balanced between British and Continental trades were likely to be indifferent to the question of independence. However, unlike the other two options, declaring neutrality in the revolution presented significant expected costs. This is because those who declared themselves neutral left themselves vulnerable to attacks—on their selves and their property—from both of the contending parties in the revolution; as such, they would suffer costs irrespective of which party had the upper hand at any point in time. They would therefore have expected to incur costs notwithstanding the uncertainty over the conflict's eventual outcome. That this cost was almost certainly expected after the declaration of independence is evident from Jackson Turner Main's observation that soon after the adoption of the first Continental Association, the committees of enforcement "tried to make everyone sign the Association, published names of those who refused as enemies of their country, and saw to it that the agreement was obeyed, by force if necessary." A neutral person would have been faced with a predicament even before the declaration of independence: "If the British government threatened his liberty from one side, fellow colonists threatened it from another."[62]

For these reasons, merchants' willingness to publicly remain neutral was likely to vary according to the extent of expected violence—from both the British and the patriots—toward those declaring themselves as such. So where potentially neutral merchants reasonably expected retaliation from either side, they would be more likely to declare their allegiance to one side or the other. But an additional set of factors would determine the side.

All other things being equal, neutral merchants were likely to ally with the side having an upper hand in the war. But if such evaluations could not be made, their choice of whom to support would depend on the dominant sentiment in their immediate social context (e.g., their town, city, county). The costs of neutrality would then be directly proportional to the probability of hostile actions from partisans on either side of the independence question, and this probability would rise with the number of people that strongly held either view. Assuming that the expected net costs or benefits of independence before the consideration of these factors is zero, it follows that neutrality was likely to be a stable position if (1) the course of the war was unclear and (2) either neutrality was the overwhelming sentiment in the merchants' immediate social context or the partisans of one position were equally balanced by the partisans of the other.[63]

The evidence that is available generally supports this explanation for merchant choices, bearing out the aggregate prediction. Southern merchants—a relatively small group to begin with—overwhelmingly became loyalists and either left the colonies or relocated to British/loyalist-controlled areas.[64] Among the merchants of the middle and northern colonies, smugglers, those doing business in continental Europe and the West Indies, and those who had earlier participated in the colonial agitations tended to declare themselves for independence.[65]

There is also some evidence in favor of this explanation of the determinants of neutrality. Studies have noted thriving pockets of neutrality in New York in general (i.e., not just among merchants), which, in turn, could be explained by the relatively equal balance between patriots and loyalists in the state as a whole.[66] For example, Joseph Tiedmann finds that out of a sample of 3,074 residents in Queens County, 1,855, or about 60 percent, were neutral, while about 27 percent were loyalist and about 13 percent Whig.[67] When these numbers are broken down by wealth, about 50 percent of those whose total wealth was estimated to be over £1,000 were neutral, about 36 percent were Tories, and only about 11 percent were Whig.[68] We do not know if the wealthy were all merchants, but it was undoubtedly easier for wealthy people to be neutral when the surrounding sentiment was also overwhelmingly neutral, which here can be explained by the relative balance of forces between the patriots and loyalists in the state. To the extent that merchants were equally distributed among the wealthy—which would obviously be an assumption—the case of Queens County supports my explanation of the behavior of neutral merchants, although it does not explain their neutrality to begin with. This point should not be overemphasized, however, or treated as definitive evidence of widespread neutrality among merchants of New York: none of these more general studies are about merchants in particular, and therefore one cannot make reliable inferences about divisions among merchants from the extent of loyalism in general.

Merchants who stood to gain from the revolution and consequently eventually declared their support for independence were dependent on the emerging rulers. This is because their futures as merchants were now crucially contingent on the patriots winning the Revolutionary War. Conversely, the total number of merchants who stood to gain from the revolution should always be evaluated in relation to the new rulers' requirements for resources to fulfill their immediate needs: since the resources needed for winning the war could not have been reliably forecast, rulers had to ensure that this particular group would be large enough to meet the maximum predicted costs of war. Rulers could have gone about this in two ways. First, they could have solicited interest-bearing loans from individual merchants and hoped that there would be enough takers. A second way would have been to seek loans from preexisting or newly constituted collectivities of merchants. This latter strategy had the virtue of ensuring the coordinated—as opposed to discrete and less mutually dependent—participation of a large number of merchants. From the merchants' perspective, too, a collective effort had some important advantages over many separate, individual efforts. Such coordination had the important virtue of reducing the risk to individual merchants; indeed, merchants knew of and widely practiced such collective risk-reducing behavior long before the revolution, especially in their long-distance trade ventures.

Negotiation and the Emergence of a Credit Market

Though the force of circumstances—specifically, mutual dependence or equal power—made cooperation between rulers and merchants highly likely, the exact terms of this cooperation were far from decided. Merchants had to be reasonably confident of recovering their loaned capital, in the event of independence, and preferably augmenting it. Barring flagrant miscalculations, therefore, rulers had every incentive to assure merchants of the reliability of their investment in the revolution. Merchants, in turn, would have wanted a credible commitment, in the words of North and Weingast, on the part of the rulers toward the repayment of any loans. Again, this presumes that merchants believed that rulers had the *ability* to ensure the repayment of loans in the future, needing only to be assured of their *willingness* to do so. Merchants believed that once independence was achieved, their investments would pay off, as long as future rulers did not present obstruction (indeed, that they would not was partly their reason for supporting independence). They required rulers both to promise and to take actual steps that would ensure the fulfillment of this promise in the future.[69]

One way of reassuring merchants would have been to allow them to collectively handle and manage currency issues and all aspects of monetary policy in general, thus effectively privatizing the monetary system. This, in turn, would entail decisions about the proper definition of "money" as well as its supply and value. Merchant control over this aspect of the economy would ensure that rulers committed not to devalue debt—indeed, that they completely ceded any ability to do so. These steps could be combined with the additional one of depositing government revenues with merchant collectivities.

Though rulers and capital holders were interdependent, it took rulers some time to realize their predicament and consequently institutionalize this mutual dependence in the form of the cooperative relationship. Similarly, it took merchants some time to perceive the necessity of acting collectively to help the movement they supported if they wanted to reap the benefits of independence, even though some of them were individually involved in supplying the army.[70] Four years elapsed before some of the new elites of the United States realized that without collective action with merchants they were facing financial disaster. The Continental Congress and the individual provincial assemblies had issued currency to finance the war, but if precipitous depreciation was any indication, no merchant capital holder was willing to accept it, especially since the notes carried neither any interest nor credible guarantees of redemption. By 1780, it was generally accepted on the part of the new U.S. political elite that this method of financing the war was a miserable failure.[71]

It was therefore not surprising that the more radical faction in the Continental Congress—generally comprising southern planters—gave way to moderates from the mercantile colonies, much to the radicals' chagrin. At the same time, even the radical Thomas Paine realized that "when the means must be drawn from the country . . . unless the wealthier part throw in their aid, public measures must go heavily on."[72] The moderate or conservative members of the Congress, present due to the fact that legislators sympathetic to merchants' views of monetary policy had managed to temporarily regain control over the important provincial assemblies of the middle and northern colonies, sought to reorient war finance. In the aftermath of two conventions, the assemblies of the various commercial provinces took a collective decision to reign in currency issuances.[73]

It was not coincidental that the events described above were taking place at the same time that merchants were organizing in relatively large numbers, explicitly to provide financial aid to war efforts.[74] Philadelphia merchants who had four years earlier declared their support for the revolution were the first to act. In March 1780, ninety-seven merchants, led by Thomas Willing, Robert Morris, and James Wilson, established a bank to supply and transport rations to the army. Almost all of these merchants had supported the patriots in Philadelphia in the years leading up to the revolution.[75] The Continental Congress took their offer and in return directed the Board of the Treasury to deposit as security all foreign aid received, not to exceed £150,000.[76] It also agreed to assist the bank with as much money as could be spared and authorized the Board to borrow on the credit of the bank.[77] This Pennsylvania Bank would in a year make way for the Bank of North America, the first chartered institution of its kind. Similar mobilizations of merchants, though on a smaller scale, were also happening in New England.[78]

The members and administrators of the newly constituted executive departments, most notably the Department of Finance, were determined to put U.S. finance on a sound footing, where "sound" implied that certain financial policies had to be taken out of the grasp of elected bodies and made the overwhelming province of private financial institutions like commercial banks. Therefore men such as Robert Morris—merchant, financier, and the first secretary of the

Department of Finance—were well aware that the key to winning merchants' enduring confidence was to eventually deprive legislatures of the ability to control the total stock of money in the economy. Morris's long-term objective was to completely replace all other kinds of government-issued paper with bank notes, which would be backed by specie: initially about $400,000, but eventually far more.[79]

Yet the Continental Congress had no power to prohibit the individual assemblies from issuing currency, and this severely restricted the extent to which such plans could be carried out. All Morris could do was send letters to the governors of the individual colonies directing them to take the necessary steps.

Nonetheless, most subscribers of the Pennsylvania Bank transferred to the new Bank of North America. The state assemblies of Connecticut, Rhode Island, Pennsylvania, New York, and Massachusetts granted it charters of incorporation, with the latter two giving it a monopoly for the duration of the war. The Bank of North America proved to be reasonably successful both in its operation and, more importantly, in being an example that subsequently encouraged other provinces to form more institutions of its kind. Specifically, it incentivized merchants from other provinces to come together to form banks. Indeed, the Bank of North America was directly associated with the establishment of similar institutions in New York and Massachusetts.[80]

The war had led to a situation in which many of the provincial assemblies were simultaneously compelled to refrain temporarily from exercising some of their monetary powers. But unless they were to relinquish these powers altogether, there was always the danger of endless negotiations and renegotiations of the terms of cooperation (depending on the historical circumstances) in the future. The arrangement, in other words, was quite unstable, since it could break down with a change in the composition of the assemblies or many other changes in the circumstances. Additionally, since under the Articles of Confederation there could not be a binding agreement applicable to all assemblies, negotiations would have to proceed on a province-by-province basis. The other possibility was the abrogation of the Articles of Confederation, which would enable a more centralized negotiation process. However, neither of these two possibilities affects the basic logic of the explanatory framework (which envisages a negotiation between a single group of rulers and another unitary group of capital holders): it merely implies that in contrast to the situation under the Confederation, the locus of negotiation would be different.

There was some variation in the interaction between banks and the assemblies or authorities of the various states in the 1780s. In the northern and middle states, the relationship ranged from accommodation and cooperation without complete privatization (in New York) to initial cooperation and then conflict, eventually ending in a compromise between banks and authorities that still did not include complete privatization (in Pennsylvania) and finally in cooperation, in the form of complete privatization (in Massachusetts). Among the southern states, only Maryland had a bank, and it and Virginia were the only southern states that were on specie standard (i.e., did not issue fiat currency).[81]

Meanwhile, a parallel movement on the part of some political elites and merchant-creditors to establish a powerful federal government received considerable momentum due to Shay's Rebellion in Massachusetts. The immediate consequence of the rebellion was the suspension of debt-funding programs in Massachusetts, which, in turn, helped to mobilize merchant opinion in favor of "the expediency of increasing the powers of Congress."[82]

This meant that the negotiation process between merchant capital holders and governing elites was transferred to the federal level. As the locus of authority began to shift from the states to the federal government, so did the locus of negotiations and the institutionalization of cooperation. That the locus shifted as the part of a larger and more encompassing reform project is, strictly speaking, irrelevant to the framework, but that the institutionalization took place is obviously of fundamental importance.

The Constitution and its ratification involved myriad issues and multiple points of negotiation, but observing the process through the lenses of the explanatory framework allows us to appreciate some of the reasons for the strong support the document received among prominent merchants. One reason is found in article 1, section 10, of the Constitution, which prohibited all state assemblies from issuing currency. When read along with the Tenth Amendment, which denied any power to the federal government not explicitly granted to it, and granted to the states (or to the "people") all power not explicitly denied to them, this cleared the way for chartered banks to take over monetary functions in the economy. Once ratified, this particular clause would exclude all but the set of actors with the willingness and ability to form chartered institutions called commercial banks from having a direct influence on one part of the economy.

Though it would be extremely difficult to separate this one issue from the larger nationalist project, we can gain some insights into the preferences of the participants in the Philadelphia convention, since they voted on each issue separately. With thirty-nine delegates voting, the vote outlawing all kinds of state currency passed with the overwhelming majority of thirty-three in favor and six against. This was the most one-sided vote among those conducted on the sixteen "salient" issues.[83] Representatives from the commercial provinces (i.e., the middle and northern provinces) voted in favor almost without exception.[84] Votes on most of the other issues were quite close. The only vote that approached a similar level of unanimity was one that gave the national government the responsibility for protecting the states from invasion as well as from internal violence when requested by the states to do so. This vote, at thirty-two for and nine against, was very similar to the one about currency, and although accurate lists associating each delegate with votes is not available, Robert McGuire's estimates suggest that there was considerable overlap between those voting in favor of the two measures.[85] Taken together, these two votes, more than any other vote in the convention, exemplify the basic terms of agreement between capital holders and rulers who saw a strong federal government as the best means of maintaining external autonomy and hierarchy. Again, this does not imply that the terms of cooperation necessarily had to be institutionalized at the federal level; it implies that whatever the locus of negotiation, these two elements were highly likely to be represented, and the currency matter (prohibiting state currency) explicitly so.

Unfortunately a similar analysis cannot be carried out for the state ratification process, since delegates voted not on specific issues but on the Constitution as a whole. As a result it would be difficult to equate support for the specific monetary clause with support for the whole, even if it is demonstrated that merchant capital holders generally supported the Constitution. Nonetheless, even otherwise antifederalist merchants generally supported the monetary clause of the Constitution, thus lending some credibility to the counterfactual that even without a movement toward a stronger federal government, reform of the monetary system would have been on the agenda.[86]

The federal government inherited all the outstanding debts of the old Congress and was still in need of resources to meet short-term interest payments. From Treasury Secretary Alexander Hamilton's perspective (and that of his predecessor Morris), the debt was not necessarily a problem. Both Hamilton and Morris had earlier noted the importance of debt in creating a more powerful and centralized national government. Speculation in public debt, which, including the principal and the interest accrued, came to approximately $40,400,000 ($27,400,000 in principal and $13,000,000 in interest), had also in the meantime created the rudiments of a market in government securities. Owing to his closeness to many of the major players in this incipient market, Hamilton could not fail to appreciate the fundamental importance of such markets in meeting the government's resource requirements in the future. Hamilton's plan was to convert all state debts into federal securities.[87] This would not only increase the size of the federal debt market but also establish the new federal government as the chief borrower and, by implication, negotiating partner.

Concomitant with the plan for the assumption of state debt, Hamilton also proposed a national bank that would cooperate specifically with the federal government. His plan was to draw prominent debt holders and existing merchant-bankers into this particular national venture. These were clearly efforts at institutionalizing cooperation at the level of the federal government rather than at the level of the states. This becomes clearer in Hamilton's insistence that the bank should be private and not responsible to Congress for its day-to-day operations and policies as well as the reasons he offers for this particular institutional arrangement:

> To attach full confidence to an institution of this nature, it appears to be an essential ingredient in its structure, that it shall

be under a *private* not a *public* direction—under the guidance of *individual interest*, not of *public policy*; which would be supposed to be, and, in certain emergencies, under a feeble or too sanguine administration, would really be, liable to being too much influenced by *public necessity*. The suspicion of this would, most probably, be a canker that would continually corrode the vitals of the credit of the bank, and would be most likely to prove fatal in those situations in which the public good would require that they should be most sound and vigorous. It would, indeed, be little less than a miracle, should the credit of the bank be at the disposal of the Government, if, in a long series of time, there was not experienced a calamitous abuse of it.[88]

Hamilton recognized that prohibiting states from issuing currency would not achieve its intended aims if the new bank were subservient to the government. There was always the danger that the "public" could reassert or claim control over the monetary system through banks, thus defeating the very purpose of privatizing the system. He realized that a credible commitment was necessary if he was going to mobilize support among merchants in favor of the bank. That is exactly the reason why he points out that if a bank were under public direction, it "would be supposed to be . . . liable to being too much influenced by public necessity." A moment's reflection should alert us to the identity of the actors who would suppose that a publicly run bank would be "liable to being too much influenced by public necessity." The whole discussion already assumed that the paper of the bank would be receivable as revenues and receipts—in other words, provide a circulatory medium—and that the government would deposit its revenues in the bank. Most merchants in the middle and the northern states, as well as chief bankers and creditors (the three groups are highly overlapping), agreed with Hamilton's plans—which quite possibly was made in consultation with some of them in the first place. Their support is evidenced by a petition presented to the Senate in the name of the public creditors, effusively praising Hamilton's bank plan about six days after Hamilton presented it.[89]

The plan for the national bank was likewise successful in attracting both creditors and merchant-bankers. In Congress, the bank had strong support in both the House and the Senate among members representing the northern and middle commercial states.[90] The subscribers to the new bank included existing banks, members of Congress, other state governments, and other chartered entities such as colleges. The connection of the first Bank of the United States with its predecessors is apparent from the list of directors and stockholders of the new bank. Thomas Willing, its most prominent director and the first president of the Bank of North America, became the president. William Bingham, his son-in-law and "a founder and director of the Bank of North America, became one of the most influential directors of the First Bank of the United States. . . . Jeremiah Wadsworth, who became a director of the Bank of the United States, represented influences leading down both from the Bank of North America and the Bank of New York."[91] Fritz Redlich summarizes the basic point that "the banks [that were] started between 1784 and 1791 (the Bank of New York, the Massachusetts Bank, the First Bank of the United States and the Bank of Maryland in Baltimore) were set up more or less under the influence of the Bank of North America and can be considered as a second crop of banks."[92]

The formation of the first Bank of the United States should therefore be considered part of the process that began with the declaration of independence and the resulting interdependence between rulers seeking independence and merchants. Though the process of cooperation resulted in the institutionalization of a financial system and capital market consisting of money markets (i.e., banking systems) and stock markets (markets for debt instruments), many details about the nature of this market were yet to be determined. What would be the rules governing banking—for example, what would the entry requirements be? These and allied issues had important implications for the price and nature of money and were central to some of the most consequential political-economic disputes of the nineteenth-century United States.

4

Merchants, Bankers,

and Rulers

States, Money, and Credit in India

I N CHAPTER 1, I argued that certain kinds of colonial relationships were special cases of the more general proposition that when rulers have the advantage vis-à-vis capital holders in the power relationship, they have no necessary incentive to make the kinds of costly concessions that lead to the emergence of institutionalized money and credit systems. Any cooperation that emerges is likely to be relatively unstable, owing to its sensitivity to factors such as rulers' discount rates and any kind of changes in personnel, including governing elites. The case of the prerevolutionary United States showed how certain specific kinds of power asymmetries underlie colonial situations that are detrimental to the emergence of institutionalized public credit and private money markets. This chapter demonstrates that a certain kind of colonial situation is a special case that can be subsumed under the more general proposition. Notwithstanding vast differences in the general setting and especially in the nature of the political institutions, the outcome was essentially similar: in neither the precolonial nor colonial Indian states did an institutionalized or state-connected money and credit system develop. To argue for the relevance of the theoretical framework for the case of India, this chapter also shows that (a) the hypothetical was a demonstrable possibility due to the extensive presence of merchants and bankers throughout the subcontinent who dealt in a variety of credit instruments and

(b) the precise counterfactual was a realistic possibility at a certain juncture in the sense that relevant actors were both aware of it and in a position to implement it.

A historical accident during the establishment of the East India Company state allows one to consider the counterfactual possibility that an integrated (i.e., including indigenous bankers and merchants), state-supported financial system *could have* emerged—and relevant actors were aware of such a possibility—but for the absence of certain crucial factors underlined in the theoretical argument. A financial system that included native financial capital holders and tied their networks to the colonial state—much as the subscribers to the Crown's loans in England were organized in the Bank of England and incorporated into the state, and the funders of the Revolutionary War in the United States contributed to the formation of its state-supported money and credit system—was arguably the most (collectively) efficient solution to some of the state's initial monetary problems. Moreover, one of the EIC's principal economic advisers suggested precisely this solution. The Company state instead chose the arguably less socially efficient and more tortuous strategy of actively eroding the property rights of native merchant-bankers and moneychangers. My theoretical argument anticipates this outcome, especially since one of its clear implications is that the power relationship between rulers and capital holders determines whether or not the collectively efficient solution necessarily obtains.

All this is done in theoretical rather than chronological order, in two parts.[1] First, I show that something akin to the counterfactual scenario—the emergence of a state-connected money and credit system—was a real possibility that was actually presented as the most efficient solution to the colonial governors tasked with addressing some of the problems arising out of the economic transformations following the emergence of EIC rule. Second, I argue that the failure of this possibility to become reality can be traced directly to the structure of the relationship between (foreign) rulers and (native) capital holders, since rulers did not have any incentive to make the kinds of concessions that could lead to the emergence of an institutionalized financial system. Moreover, this failure was itself a further exacerbation of a situation where the precolonial state was only sporadically involved in the functioning of private money and credit markets. This was due, again, to the prevailing power relationship between native rulers—first the Mughal state and then, upon its gradual disintegration, its provincial successors—and financiers, in which rulers had no stable or long-term incentives to accord special protection to the interests of capital holders. Ironically, it was precisely this situation that led native bankers and merchants to assist the EIC initially in its struggles against native rulers. And though their financial assistance to the Company was rational in the short term, it proved fatal in the medium to long term as the new rulers drastically curtailed or eliminated their property rights. Moreover, as the theoretical framework would predict, the property rights of native financial capital holders diminished as those of native landed elites were enhanced.

THE COUNTERFACTUAL

In the mid-1780s, Charles Cornwallis arrived in India as the third governor general of the Company-ruled "presidency" of Bengal, charged with regularizing Company revenues, fighting corruption in administration, and putting government finances on a sound footing.[2] Despite acquiring one of the richest and most lucrative provinces of the subcontinent, the Company was having major problems in accumulating the riches that its directors in London had expected.[3] Part of the problem was widespread corruption among Company servants, who essentially plundered the Bengal treasury and subsequently diverted the revenue collected, soon after the military defeat of the local ruler.[4] A related component was the scarcity of currency—chiefly silver, which was dominant in the subcontinent. The various European companies trading in India, including the British EIC, had hitherto imported bullion in order to pay for Indian goods. The Company ceased this practice after its acquisition of Bengal, since it expected revenues to obviate the need for bullion imports. Yet the Bengal revenues, enormous as they were, did not quite suffice.[5] In addition to the aforementioned plunder, the opening of trade with China, which required silver exports from Bengal, resulted in major scarcity of the payment medium.[6]

Cornwallis's predecessors had attempted to relieve currency scarcity by trying to introduce bimetallism and, when that failed, a uniform currency, to replace the many varieties in circulation.[7] One of the major reasons that both measures failed was that they went directly against the interests of local bankers and moneychangers (*shroffs* or *sarrafs*). Indeed, such measures—especially the introduction of a uniform currency—were aimed specifically at completely repudiating the property rights of these native financial capital holders. Yet this proved to be a difficult task. Even though the Company had become the sole government of Bengal, the task of effectively controlling its economy was complicated by the fact that the credit and monetary system was highly decentralized, which was partially a result of the earlier disintegration of centralized Mughal rule. The total amount of payment medium in the economy, including its supply and definition, was immediately subject to the activities of numerous bankers and merchants who controlled and operated mints. The Company state also had some mints directly under its control, but did not have a monopoly over coinage. Although it played an important role, it was only one participant among others in the money and credit system.

Thus, when the Company wrested control from the *nawab* (honorific title of the rulers) of Bengal, it also secured control over one of the largest mints of the province. But this did not grant it monopoly status, since the Company still did not have control over most of the mints. This meant that the attempts of the various governors general at currency control could be thwarted by the actions of *shroffs* who held currency stocks.[8] Since the Company lacked a monopoly over these stocks, its other option was to use its monopoly over organized violence to compel *shroffs* to follow its dictates. But, though it was clearly the only coercive authority in the province, the Company did not yet possess the requisite administrative capacity to *effectively* enforce its authoritative commands and monitor the activities of *shroffs* within a territory around the combined size—in population as well as area—of all the German-speaking European states at the time. There was, however, a third and arguably more efficient policy option to ameliorate currency shortage and the various problems arising out of it in the long term: working in concert with—rather than against the interests of—native bankers and merchants. This last solution, as I discuss further below, would have required relatively little administrative capacity while inducing the willing cooperation of the local merchants and bankers. Instead, the state chose to follow a longer process that was more arduous and, arguably, inefficient.

In the 1760s, for instance, Robert Clive sought to introduce gold in addition to silver coins. He was assuming that there were large private hoards of gold in India, whose owners could be induced to part with it at an advantageous exchange rate. He therefore sought to set the value of a gold coin at about fourteen times the value of a silver coin, which was an overvaluation of about 17.5 percent relative to the prevailing market rate. The Company's governing council even passed an injunction promising severe punishment for any deviation from the exchange rate, and included it in a public notice. Yet silver disappeared from circulation, and gold currency passed at substantial discount even in Calcutta, the seat of the Company government.[9] Company officials held *shroffs* as primarily responsible for this outcome.[10] Clive's successor, Harry Verelst, tried something similar but with some additional safeguards, such as placing Company functionaries in selected mints. Yet gold was again overvalued relative to the market rate, and the upshot was the same as before.

Finally, the Company changed its strategy and sought to establish a single, uniform currency throughout Bengal, which implied the demonetization of many existing currencies. Though the silver coin predominated in the region, it passed at various rates of discount once it passed three years from its date of minting (which was inscribed on the coin). The newer coins were called *sicca* rupees, while those more than three years old were called *sanouts*. *Shroffs* regulated the rates of discount (called *batta*) between *siccas* and *sanouts* of various dates. The Company's plan, first tried under Verelst in the early 1770s, was to prohibit the distinction between *siccas* and *sanouts* and establish *siccas*, coined at mints sanctioned by the Company, as the sole currency.[11]

But again, the Company had neither a monopoly over the stock of existing *siccas* nor sufficient administrative capacity—including effective control over mints situated far from Calcutta—to ensure compliance with its dictates. Thus, any deviation of the officially mandated rate of exchange (between the old currency and the new replacements) from the prevailing market rate could create arbitrage opportunities. Indeed, the very market rate could be set by native bankers to their advantage, and at the expense of the Company. These problems led the government to abandon its first attempt at establishing uniform currency in 1771.[12]

At the failure of the first attempt, the government determined that the major problem for its plans was the weak supervision of mints situated outside Calcutta. It thus did the next best thing by closing two major mints in Dacca and Patna. This was soon followed by the closure of yet another mint, this time in Murshidabad in 1777.[13] Verelst's successor, Warren Hastings, then issued an order prohibiting all kinds of coin discounting. The government further stipulated that it would accept only Calcutta *sicca* rupees in payment and that these would be the only legal tender.[14]

This attempt failed also, because it proved highly unrealistic for those making payments to the government to travel to Calcutta to exchange their coins for current *siccas.* For the same reason, people continued to make other payments in older currencies. Closure of the mints allowed *shroffs* to buy up large stocks of *siccas* and sell them at a premium. Most importantly, the Company's administrative capacity had not increased by much during this time. Thus, bankers in Patna, for instance, continued to distinguish between, and hence discount, the various currencies. The government retaliated by threatening dire consequences unless bankers in Patna conformed to orders that would effectively forcefully devalue their stocks of currency.[15] Though this worked for a short period, other problems such as the lack of conveniently situated mints complicated the task of establishing the Calcutta *sicca* as the standard currency.

Cornwallis kept up this war of attrition between the government and native bankers when, having learned from previous failures, he resumed efforts at establishing a uniform currency. Thus, he declared *sicca* rupees coined after 1791 as the only official currency, reopened the closed mints under closer supervision, and moved the Calcutta mints to larger facilities (that included storage), which allowed for exchanges between older currency and the new at all the branches of the mint. This was followed, in 1794, by yet another order stipulating that only Company *siccas* would be accepted and issued at treasuries, and that the coins minted at all the mints should be identical in design, metal content, and weight.[16] Two further factors assisted Cornwallis in this endeavor. First, closure of the mints outside Calcutta probably drained *shroffs*' stocks of silver *siccas*.[17] Second, and perhaps more importantly, war with the Kingdom of Mysore in 1789 had allowed Cornwallis to import a large amount of silver from Europe throughout the 1790s.[18]

Cornwallis's administration finally succeeded in establishing the silver *sicca* as the official government currency. Though not the only one, since the government would intermittently try to introduce gold alongside silver, the *sicca* would henceforth be acceptable for all government payments and transactions. Its effect on purely nongovernmental transactions was far more mixed. There is some evidence that despite the order, unauthorized coins were still in circulation, and moneychangers continued their business in various districts of Bihar as late as the 1820s.[19] Nonetheless, the Company government did manage to achieve its major goals with regards to currency. It established itself as the sole minting and financial authority in the province and further solidified its predominant role in high finance, thereby excluding all native bankers and merchants. This began the process of the division of the Indian capital market into what John Maynard Keynes was to characterize a century later as the "European" money market and the "Indian" market.[20] The distributional implications of these developments were quite clear to contemporaries. Indeed, in sharp contrast to native bankers, British merchants consistently welcomed the government's policy measures, especially the demonetization of preexisting currencies.[21]

Though the government achieved one of its major goals, the process took close to forty years and came at a high cost to the economy of Bengal (in terms of lost trade, among other things) and, indeed, to the government itself.[22] Yet since 1772, there existed an alternative policy proposal, which would have introduced a uniform currency and simultaneously greatly mitigated the shortage, much more efficiently (insofar as efficiency is a function of time). As some economic historians of India have noted, this proposal appeared in a report that was circulated, and hence widely known, among Company policy makers. Yet an explanation for why it was never adopted—even as some other unrelated suggestions, contained in the same document, were—remains to be advanced.[23] The remainder of this chapter, therefore, first outlines the contours of the proposal and the alternative financial system it would probably have created and then traces the failure of this alternative outcome to the power relationship between the state and indigenous capital holders.

The section above briefly noted the difficulties the Company faced in effectively enforcing its monetary dictates, observing that much of the difficulty arose from the recalcitrance of indigenous bankers and moneychangers. As Company officials often noted, *shroffs* were adept at defeating any measure "that was likely to injure their gains." So adept, in fact, that their machinations were likened to the "talents of Sir Isaac Newton and Mr. [John] Locke."[24] The government persisted in its efforts instead of cooperating with native bankers. Yet one of the Company's principal advisors in England, Sir James Steuart—who was also one of the most eminent economists of his time—had suggested precisely this solution to the Company's currency problems.[25]

Steuart suggested that the Company could increase circulation and, in doing so, reduce shortages by introducing paper currency (though bills of exchange, both native and European, were common, these did not have the status of legal tender). However, this was not all: he could have suggested that paper should circulate as currency only among Europeans, to the exclusion of native bankers, but he insisted that native bankers and merchants be included in the larger plan. Indeed, he contended that paper currency should be issued and discounted by banks controlled collectively by combinations of both native and European bankers.

Steuart made his suggestions on banking and credit in the form of a report that circulated widely among the governors of the EIC. The second part of his report deals specifically with the proposal for paper credit and banks, while the first part is about the various theories of currency value applied to the situation in Bengal. In language reminiscent of one justifying the quasi-private nature of the Bank of England or Hamilton defending the charter of the first Bank of the United States, it said, "The principle on which this branch of credit is grounded, is totally incompatible with sovereign power. It is founded on private utility, and it has even occasion for a superior authority to keep it within bounds."[26] The reason, predictably, was that if the state established its own bank, and if the bank managed to corner most of the specie of Bengal, the government would be tempted to expend all or most of it for defense, thus depriving the paper currency of any backing.[27] Steuart then goes on to propose a bank that, similar to the Bank of England, would be capitalized at the amount lent to the Company. The entire fund loaned to the Company could then be

> divided into shares . . . transferable as the funds are in England, bearing . . . interest . . . and an exclusive privilege may be granted to the subscribers for the same number of years [i.e., the number of years for which the debt is irredeemable], for the purpose of carrying on a banking trade; by the issuing of notes in the discounting of good bills . . . or in consideration of pledges of treasure, jewels or precious effects deposited in the Bank: or upon the mortgage of good property, and the best personal security, for such length of time as may be judged reasonable and safe: or in the purchase of gold and silver: Or lastly for advancing certain sums of money to the Company, upon the security of their annual revenue, according to the practice of the Bank of England.[28]

Further, "under these and such other regulations that the East India Company may think proper to add, this Banking Company may be laid open to natives as well as Europeans."[29] That he was fully aware of the consequences of this advice is abundantly clear from what he writes next:

> It is impossible to say what operations will be carried on by the Bank, and how far it may in time extend its credit. It may for this purpose open offices in all the principal cities of Bengal; which will be admirably well calculated for calling in and re-coining all the old and unequal coin. *The shroffs will naturally become proprietors, and will lend their assistance in this particular, which will be a douceur for them.* They will be employed in a trade something like what they now carry on; but it will be so fenced in proper regulations, that it will have every advantage and none of the inconveniencies of the present practice.[30]

He recognizes that in this situation there is no longer any incentive for native bankers to oppose the Company's currency measures; indeed, they would be expected to enthusiastically support them. This is because the plan would have sufficiently compensated them—especially by giving them a long-term stake in the new monetary system—for their willingness to relinquish status quo property rights. It would thus have involved extensive cooperation with native bankers. As he continues:

> It would not I think be proper to admit any person of the council to be either a governor, or a director of this Bank [he later suggests, in a different context, that an indigenous banker would be a good candidate for the governor of the bank]; but I think it would be expedient to secure the property of the fund for the payment of the bank paper, exclusive of all other engagements the Banking Company may contract. If we consider the rate of money in Bengal, there will be perhaps 8 per cent on the Bank stock, and 8 per cent more upon discounting loans &c. [B]oth together will produce so great an emolument as to engage people of wealth and property in the banking scheme: Besides, the very notion of standing upon a solid and independent footing, will be extremely flattering to many of the natives. *And as the establishment is planned upon the same principles as the Bank of England, it is natural to suppose that it may produce similar effects in supporting the credit of the Company on one hand, and in being supported by the Company on the other.*[31]

Steuart here describes, almost exactly, the theoretical counterfactual to what actually occurred in Bengal. The consummate technocrat, he did not consider whether the Company had any incentive to carry out his plans or whether the Company's creditors in London or the British government could countenance a situation in which native bankers would be in a position to dictate the monetary policy of the new government of Bengal. The problem, in his mind, was clearly defined: how to overcome the currency shortage, while simultaneously promoting a uniform currency in Bengal in a manner that would greatly simplify economic transactions. He imagined that the government would be open to doing whatever would result in the most efficient outcome, where "efficiency" would be defined in strictly utilitarian terms relative to the clearly described problem to be solved. Indeed, his solution was perhaps the most efficient one *if one agreed with the definition of the problem.* However, the basic problem, from the Company's perspective, was how to standardize the currency and increase circulation while at the same time establishing and maintaining complete and sole control over the monetary situation in Bengal. They had not defeated the *nawab* and seized mints only to have to relinquish some of their power over the Bengal economy to local bankers and merchants.

The very structure of the relationship between native financial capital holders and the state precluded mutual cooperation and hence the outcome Steuart envisaged. In effect, the new rulers had a distinct advantage in the power relationship, which allowed them to completely disregard the preferences of native capital holders. The state's advantage, in turn, was predicated on its relationships with native landed elites and then, more importantly, with the London financial market. The lack of an institutionalized money market with mass deposit banking, or the use of contemporaneously modern fiduciary instruments that would, for instance, allow the government to manage seasonally fluctuating demands for currency, were a direct result of this dynamic. Native capital constituted the *bazaar*, the informal money and credit market: "informal" not because unorganized or minor but precisely because of the lack of state involvement.

The contrast to the state's relationship with landed elites was particularly instructive. The EIC state further strengthened the property rights of landlords by making them outright owners of land, rather than revenue collectors, ostensibly in order to maximize land revenue. Christopher Bayly expresses the historians' consensus that the famous "Permanent Settlement" giving them this status "entrench[ed] the power of zamindars or landlords . . . in the interests of stable revenue for an imperial state at war."[32]

The Mechanism and the Outcome

The Late Precolonial Background

Economic historians writing on seventeenth- to late eighteenth-century finance and credit have occasionally puzzled over the seemingly incongruous (dual) phenomena of the existence of highly sophisticated credit instruments and networks that spanned the entire subcontinent but had few systematic connections to the state. This lack of connection was in contrast to what was happening in certain European states during the same time. For example, Irfan Habib has commented on the extent and sophistication of the credit system, observing:

> From the point of view of the development of merchant capital, [the] Indian economy appears to have reached a fairly advanced stage. It is noticeable that seventeenth-century European merchants and factors [brokers/middlemen who contracted with producers] make no serious criticism of the Indian credit system, and there is little inclination to compare it unfavorably with the European, although most of its particularities, or differences, are noted.[33]

Susil Chaudhuri notes, "The merchants of Bengal, as in other parts of India, operated with their own capital and there was hardly any close financial link between the merchant and the public—a feature which was fast developing in England in the seventeenth century through the joint stock companies."[34] Thus, the nature of credit was strictly private; bankers or *sarrafs* accepted money on deposit at interest, which, in turn, facilitated the creation of book or credit money when they accepted bills from those who drew them. The bills were then entered in their books at interest and were transferable without being convertible into cash. Thus, a "large amount of book money could be created without any backing in coin or bullion, *but only on the strength of the general credit enjoyed by the sarrafs.*"[35] As the italicized part of the statement indicates, book money was acceptable only in transactions among merchants and was not endorsed or backed by the state. It was therefore fiat money, resting on private credit and bearing little direct connection to state-sanctioned money.

The common feature underlying both the lack of "financial link between the merchant and the public" and the nature of the credit described was the notable absence of the state. Indeed, the Mughal state was only sporadically involved—as, among other things, a guarantor and contract enforcer—in the private money and credit market.

In Mughal provinces with high density of financial capital holders, merchants' associations, or *mahajans*, were largely autonomous from the state insofar as setting market rules, interest rates, or production standards was concerned.[36] Rulers' indifference, in other words, had two implications for merchants. On one hand, it ensured that they could formulate their own laws of exchange in spheres that did not concern rulers, but, on the other, it severely handicapped them since, unlike their European counterparts, they did not have the consistent and reliable backing of the coercive force of the state. The Mughal state was never *their* state and Mughal laws were never *their* laws—in fact, there were no Mughal laws governing exchange and commerce. This is a sharp contrast to the case in England, where merchants' codes and practices were incorporated into the common law in the eighteenth century.[37]

This also meant that state finances were quite independent from the activities of merchants and bankers. Not only did the state have independent treasuries; high-ranking state officials rarely used existing merchants' bills of exchange (also known as *hundis*) for fund transfers between various regional treasuries, relying instead on official state bills.[38] Furthermore, at the height of its power (under the emperors Akbar and Aurangzeb), the state maintained strict control over imperial mints. Therefore, despite the fact that the mints worked on the principle of "free coinage"—that is, anybody could get bullion converted to official currencies upon paying a fee—the state could regulate the money supply (insofar as anyone could), owing to its monopoly over minting.[39] The state exercised this prerogative on several occasions—by, among other things, increasing the value of currency by fiat—against the wishes of bankers and moneychangers.[40]

This state of affairs could be traced to the fact that by far the largest source of revenue for the Mughal state was tied to land. Other revenues barely registered in official accounting (see Appendix 4.1). Mughal rulers therefore never considered merchants and bankers stable or *necessary* sources of state finance, even during wars. Indeed, the state itself was a major lender to its nobility and high-ranking officers, and provincial-level state elites combined their governing functions with extending credit, including to merchants.[41] In the language of the theoretical framework elaborated earlier, rulers, having a clear advantage in the power relationship, did not need to make any special dispensation to the interests of financial capital holders. Again, a corollary—and contrast—to rulers' relationship with capital holders was that *zamindars* (akin to landlords) were considered agents of the state who directly collected land revenues and passed it on to higher officials, keeping a portion for themselves. Indeed, the *zamindar* designation, which predated the Mughals and connoted many different kinds of property rights that varied over time and region, became equated with the right to collect taxes directly. This right was subject to seizure only upon a payment by the state to compensate for the *zamindar*'s exclusion from a particular piece of land.[42] Unlike merchants and bankers, *zamindars* were incorporated directly into the state and hence received its protection, and this even created a market for *zamindari* rights.[43]

This description should not imply the acceptance of a picture of the "Mughal state as an Oriental despotism, 'monopolizing trades at the drop of a hat, fleecing merchants at breakfast, and generally carrying on as a public nuisance.'"[44] As Ashin Das Gupta observes, Indian merchants and bankers "neither enjoyed the patronage of . . . [the] state nor . . . [went] in fear of . . . [the] government."[45] For one thing, they dominated much of the trade in the Indian Ocean through most of the sixteenth and seventeenth centuries, and numerous merchants and bankers became exceedingly wealthy—indeed, wealthy enough to be major short-term creditors of European trading companies.[46] Their financial relationship with the EIC was the principal reason why they assisted the Company during its struggles against local rulers in the aftermath of the breakdown of central Mughal rule. It was a matter of simply calculating the relative benefits, as they had been accustomed to doing in the past. There had been instances of merchants offering to compensate the Mughal emperor monetarily for damages the ruler sustained from skirmishes with Europeans in return for the emperor's agreement not to disrupt trade or escalate military confrontation with European companies.[47] The only difference was that this time the EIC was actually in a position to challenge the local ruler. This difference accounted for the deleterious long-term consequences of the new Company state for indigenous merchants and bankers.

The East India Company and the Emergence
of a Colonial Financial System

The gradual breakup of the Mughal state following the death of Emperor Aurangzeb in 1707 implied much greater autonomy for provincial rulers who had hitherto been *subahdars* (roughly, provincial administrative officers) of the emperor. However, the attendant disruption in revenue transfer mechanisms and loss of access to regional treasuries led them to reorganize the mechanisms of revenue extraction. Thus, the rulers of erstwhile Mughal *subas* (provinces) with access to large land revenues and the machinery for realizing them generally managed to continue as before. When such revenue mechanisms faced disruption, rulers had to rely on merchant-creditors and even involve them in the collection system. Yet this inclusion was merely temporary because these transitory disruptions did not change rulers' expectations of their principal long-term sources. Thus, such arrangements were not really credible in the sense defined earlier. Bankers, whom they greatly benefited, stood therefore to lose substantially in the event of a breakdown, but rulers would face only negligible costs in that same eventuality. As a result, such arrangements were unstable and sensitive to factors such as the specific identity of the ruler.[48]

The *subahdar* of the province of Bengal, Murshid Quli Khan, had originally been appointed as the *diwan* (revenue and treasury officer) by Emperor Aurangzeb. Subsequent to the emperor's death, as central Mughal rule attenuated, Murshid Quli Khan managed to combine the offices of the *subahdar* and *diwan*. In addition, he made the banking house of his friend—who had moved with him to Bengal from North India—the official banker of the rulers of Bengal and awarded the head of the bank the title of "Jagat Seth" or "Bankers of the World."[49] This was in return for the assistance that his friend Manikchand's successor, Fateh Chand, had rendered in reorganizing Bengal revenues. Every successive head of the banking house held the title until the Battle of Plassey in 1757, when the EIC seized control of the revenues.

Their official status meant that the Jagat Seth bankers had keys to the treasury and partial control over mints, which, in turn, allowed them considerable influence on exchange rates and credit flow in Bengal. Additionally, the state also accepted their deposit notes in lieu of amounts deposited by *zamindars*, and drew drafts on the house to make payments. The Jagat Seths also stood security for *zamindars'* revenue payments.[50] Yet this arrangement was not credible for the reasons noted above. The Jagat Seths were merely intermediaries who could be easily removed or replaced without much cost to the rulers, and the reason was that the state itself was never indebted to the banking house, let alone to bankers and merchants in general. Indeed, rulers explicitly refused direct financial assistance from the Jagat Seths.[51] The overwhelming majority of state revenue still depended on land that the *zamindars* directly controlled (see Appendix 4.1). Moreover, the rulers of Bengal were quite conscious of this. As N. K. Sinha has noted, "The attitude of the Subahdars from Murshid Quli to Alivardi [one of his successors] could be best expressed in the following words—'Let them [the *zamindars*] grow rich, the state will grow rich also.'"[52] As a result, merchants and bankers, unlike *zamindars*, were accorded no role in statecraft.[53]

The Jagat Seths'—and generally indigenous merchant and bankers'—relationship to the state was similar to their relationship with the EIC in one fundamental way. Even though the Company had extensive dealings with them, the EIC never considered local bankers and merchants as permanent or long-term partners. Indeed, the governors of the EIC often explicitly discouraged their merchants from seeking local credit.[54] Their reasons are not difficult to fathom. The EIC was a principal participant in the "financial revolution" in England, and was the second-largest borrower in the London financial market.[55] Moreover, the government, in return for the Company's enormous loans to the Crown, backed repeated EIC debt issues. This gave both its stockholders in London and the government a vested interest in controlling the activities of Company servants in India. Yet in return for this control, the government and stockholders had to repeatedly consent to new debt issues. Commenting on the early years of the Company state, Holden Furber remarks that without fresh issues, which allowed EIC servants in India to cash in their bills of exchange on London and thus facilitated the continued repatriation of wealth from India to Britain, English merchants "would have been forced to attempt to govern India themselves in an effort to protect their investment."[56] This expresses an interesting counterfactual involving the loss of the EIC's chief source of financial resources. As was briefly noted earlier, and is further demonstrated below, continued access to the London financial market was subsequently directly responsible for the lack of a similar financial system in India.

Nonetheless, as long as it was not in a position to challenge first the Mughal state and then its provincial successors, the EIC had to rely on the considerable resources of local merchant-bankers for bridge (or short-term) credit. Indeed, at times this short-term credit was substantially more than half the entire value of the Company's investments in Bengal.[57] No wonder, then, that some EIC merchants saw the House of the Jagat Seths—who were only the most prominent among many local bankers they dealt with—as "a great[er] Banker than all in Lombard Street jointed together."[58] The system whereby local merchant-bankers both acted as brokers and advanced short-term credit in order to finance the EIC's purchases was called the *dadni* system. And consistent with the explanation advanced here—in particular the EIC's bargaining advantage—the Company discontinued this system shortly after acquiring access to land revenues.[59]

Given the structure of these relationships, conflicts between the EIC and local rulers were manifestly against the interests of local financial capital holders. From the perspective of these bankers, it was precisely the status quo—in which the EIC at least acquiesced to the authority of local rulers—that allowed them to profit from their relationship with the Company. Their subsequent actions, especially their efforts to mediate between local rulers and the EIC in order to deescalate conflicts, clearly suggest that they were well aware of this. Yet since they were structurally powerless vis-à-vis both parties, there were clear limits on the extent to which they could influence outcomes. Moreover, the relationship between local rulers and the Company was never amicable due to certain fundamentally irreconcilable differences.

The Company was perpetually reluctant to pay duties to local rulers. As K. N. Chaudhuri wryly observes, "A trading organization that voluntarily offered £10000 to its sovereign equated a payment of £500 to an Asian Prince with political extortion."[60] The reasons for this apparent hypocrisy are easy to fathom once one realizes that the EIC was an enterprise "whose monopoly and other commercial privileges were upheld by the state largely as a result of the financial payments received by the Crown . . . [and whose] entire permanent capital of £3 million was lent to the Crown."[61] Local rulers, on the other hand, resented that the Company, unlike the Armenian and other merchants trading in Bengal, insisted on its own fortifications and army. This was a direct affront to the authority of local rulers, particularly since Company merchants were seen to be transgressing their customary roles as mere merchants who were expected to play no role in matters of governance, including order and protection.[62]

When these tensions erupted into armed conflict between the EIC and Siraj ud-Daulah, the ruler of Bengal, Siraj initially drove the Company out of its fortifications. Prominent merchants and bankers of Bengal, including the Jagat Seth, then tried to broker some sort of compromise between the *nawab* and the English that would restore the previous status quo. Siraj refused to allow the Company to trade unless it gave up its arms and fortifications.[63] Additionally, he grew suspicious of and then hostile toward the principal bankers of Bengal, including the Jagat Seths, for pleading on behalf of the Company.[64]

The subsequent decision of local merchant-bankers, including the house of the Jagat Seth, to assist the Company in bribing the *nawab*'s generals was quite rational in this context.[65] They could not influence the EIC to give up its weapons and fortifications, although they would have preferred that it did so. But they could play some part in unseating a ruler whose reign was becoming increasingly costly for them, in terms of both lost business and his increasing hostility. From their perspective, removal of this obdurate ruler would have gone a long way toward restoring the desired state of affairs. The status quo had, however, irrevocably changed in ways that were deleterious to the interests of these local bankers. Even if they had anticipated the long-term consequences of their actions, their structural situation meant that they did not have the luxury to act accordingly.

In the aftermath of the 1757 Battle of Plassey—the "mock" battle between the two armies that unseated Siraj-ud-daula—the EIC secured *zamindari* rights to some of the most lucrative districts of Bengal, in addition to exemption from all duties and taxes.[66] Its demands on local rulers, however, did not stop there. When the bribed generals who replaced Siraj refused to concede to the Company's more extravagant demands, such as to reinstitute custom duties and tax competitors after the ruler had resolved to make trade completely free within his realm, this led to yet another battle, a mere eight years after Siraj's fall.[67] The Battle of Buxar in 1765 gave the Company control over the Bengal treasury.

The implications of all this for local merchant-bankers were entirely consistent with the framework advanced here. The Jagat Seths lost control over the treasury and a major mint (they had lost their monopoly over minting privileges after 1757). More generally, as Company servants indulged in what P. J. Marshall described as large-scale looting of the Bengal coffers, erstwhile debtors to local bankers became creditors in their own right.[68] In addition to the drastic diminution in their financial property rights described above and the end of the *dadni* system after 1758, some local bankers now became deputies to British merchants.[69] And even though the Company persisted in using existing credit networks of local merchant-bankers to transfer funds all across the subcontinent during the various conflicts, this too came to an end once the EIC started establishing its own banks and other revenue transfer mechanisms.[70]

It is worth reiterating the point implicit in Furber's observation that without continued access to the London financial market, EIC merchants would have had to "govern India themselves . . . to protect their investments." My argument here is that governing India "themselves" would have entailed a kind of financial system very different from what actually eventually emerged. The financial system that did emerge was an institution whose primary purpose was to facilitate the transfer of merchants' funds from India to Britain; this fact accounted for many of its missing features (compared to other contemporaneous European systems). And all of this was directly due to the EIC government's (and after 1857, the government of India's) continued access to the London financial market and the institutional concessions that the governmental Board of Control in London extracted for this access.

Because the Company was almost immediately embroiled in a series of conflicts in various other regions of the subcontinent, revenue from lands that it acquired after 1765, though substantial, did not meet its financial requirements, and this situation continued throughout the nineteenth century (see Figure 4.1 and Appendix 4.2).[71] The Company did, however, succeed in increasing its stock prices in London and in assuring both the government and its stockholders that their faith in the Company was not misplaced.[72] Had its access to the London market not been so direct, the Company would have had to float permanent domestic debts. Indeed, the high plausibility of this counterfactual is evidenced by the fact that the flotation of domestic debts was a point of contention between the government in India and the Board of Control (of the EIC) in London.

The government in India wanted the option to float debts in pursuit of territorial expansion, while the Board's view was akin to that of a merchant organization that wanted the government to simply transfer the surplus Bengal revenue to London by applying it to trade (i.e., paying for its investments or purchases in India with the revenue).[73] Yet the expansionary conflicts made it impossible to use all the revenue toward trade, forcing the Company government to borrow from its own servants in India. However, this did not lead to anything like the creation of a market for state debts as conventionally understood. Lending to the government became just another way of transferring the savings of Company servants to London. The government offered bills of exchange payable in London after a fixed period of time, and the Company often met these obligations through further borrowing in the London market. The same drive to repatriate wealth led to the creation of "agency houses," which tapped into mainly British capital "to be invested in country trade or indigo or usurious loans to the government."[74] This was highly inconvenient for the government, since it impeded the formation of a pool of capital from which the government could draw in times of need. The government complained about this state of affairs, but the Board of Control wanted to preclude precisely what the government wanted.[75] The Board knew that the policy of debt transfer necessarily tied British merchants (and agency houses) trading in India to London and made the government in India responsive to its directions. Thus, on one hand the Board advised the EIC government against incurring too many expenses in India and issuing bills of exchange to fund them (since these debts

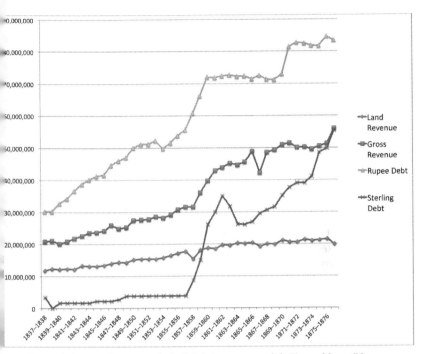

Sources: A. Banerji, *Finances in the Early Raj: Investments and the External Sector* (New Delhi: Sage, 1995), 302–303, 350; R. C. Dutt, *The Economic History of India in the Victorian Age: From the Accession of Queen Victoria in 1837 to the Commencement of the Twentieth Century* (London: Routledge and Keegan Paul, 1956), 212, 217, 373–374. *Note:* All amounts are in British pounds.

Figure 4.1. Apart from land, government monopolies in opium and salt were the other chief sources of revenue. Detailed figures for revenues from these goods are not available, but in 1858–1859 they made up about a quarter of the total revenue (Dharma Kumar, "The Fiscal System," in *The Cambridge Economic History of India*, vol. 2, *c. 1751–c. 1970*, ed. Dharma Kumar [Cambridge: Cambridge University Press, 1983], 916). The sterling debts were raised in London, while the rupee debts were raised in both India and England. The difference between the two was that the rupee securities were denominated in the Indian currency. Britain-based financial institutions and absentee British investors held both kinds of debts (R. W. Goldsmith 1983, *The Financial Development of India, 1860–1977* [New Haven, CT: Yale University Press, 1983], 41).

would eventually come back to London), but on the other hand, it never altered its policy of debt transfer.[76]

Government revenues hardly improved, and the general policy of tying India debts to London continued under many different guises throughout the nineteenth century, as did strict control of the Indian financial system from London. The Board retained the power to cancel licenses granted by the government of India to agency houses if, for example, it thought that said houses had powerful native partners.[77] The official banks in the presidencies of Bombay, Bengal, and Madras, established in the first decade of the nineteenth century, were denied commercial banking functions such as "the regulation of the whole monetary or credit system of the country or the regulation of the foreign exchange market."[78] The currency of India was strictly tied to bullion movements so that it "could be expanded only by bringing in funds from abroad, say by buying commercial bills in London or by importation of sovereigns," thus precluding such measures as fractional reserve banking.[79] This general state of affairs continued throughout the nineteenth century. As a U.S. observer noted in the early twentieth century, in India, unlike in the West, there was no "recourse to . . . arrangements" wherein "fluctuations in demands for currency [could] largely [be] met by an increase or decrease in the use of fiduciary contrivances."[80] In the second half of the nineteenth century, specialized banks called "exchange banks" were allowed to deal in foreign exchange and bullion. But most of these banks "were British, in the sense that they were incorporated in Great Britain, had their main office in London, and most of their shares were owned by British investors."[81]

Every institutional measure extracted in return for the EIC government's (and, after 1857, the British government of India's) access to the London financial market can be seen as a credible commitment made by the Company to its creditors. Vital effects of the commitment, however, were geographically displaced inasmuch as they were felt not in India but in the London financial market, contributing to its further development. Thus, capital for the infrastructural projects planned after the mutiny of 1857 was raised mainly in London. Only about 1 percent of the total capital for railway construction was raised in India. As an additional incentive for investment, the railway loans were guaranteed a minimum rate of return by the Indian government.[82] The decision to raise funds for such projects in the London market was probably partly a result of the difficulty of doing so in India, which was itself an outcome of, or endogenous to, the poor development of the Indian financial system, which in turn was the result of the decisions described above.

Native capital nonetheless did not disappear. It just retreated to the domains left to it, thus becoming a part of the informal sector. This sector—the *bazaar*—was highly organized, and had banking networks connecting every major city of India through a variety of negotiable paper, including credit notes such as the *hundi* (a bill of exchange).[83] Yet it is worth reiterating that the *bazaar* was necessarily limited in important ways. Since the state did not enforce contracts, mass deposit banking of the kind emerging in the West could not really develop. In the absence of an impersonal contract enforcer, banking was limited to networks of merchants, and thus the *bazaar* could not avail itself of individual savings in a systematic manner. It nonetheless would subsequently figure in some important developments at the turn of the century, including as a source of funds for both the first large-scale indigenous manufacturing enterprise and the Indian National Congress.[84]

THE UNITED STATES AND INDIA: SOME OBSERVATIONS

Despite many other differences, India and the prerevolutionary colonies in North America had essential similarities in light of this book's theoretical framework. In both cases, largely at the behest of British creditors, the state severely restricted what have since come to be understood as some of the basic functions and developments of the money and credit system. In situations where domestic financial capital holders were at a disadvantage in the power relationship, continued access to foreign creditors dictated the policy steps that led to the outcomes in both cases. To be sure, there were contextual differences, but these serve only to demonstrate that the same basic mechanisms operated in two different contexts to bring about similar outcomes. In the case of the prerevolutionary North American colonies, the relationship between the British state and capital holders, on one hand,

and colonial merchants on the other constituted a structure where there was little domestic impetus for the establishment of financial institutions. In India, the same outcome arose from the displacement of indigenous merchants and bankers and the establishment of policies—debt transfer, for instance—and institutions aimed specifically at precluding the emergence of a permanent pool of (expatriate British) financial capital in India. Indeed, both the Crown and British creditors wanted to prevent outcomes akin to the Revolutionary War, which had given rise to the first financial institutions in the United States. The fear, here expressed in the words of Henry Dundas, head of the Board of Control between 1784 and 1801, in a letter to Richard Wellesley, governor general of India between 1798 and 1805, was that European settlers "mixing themselves with the natives *ad libitum*, do incalculable mischief. . . . [S]uch a system, if not duly restrained and regulated, will ultimately lead to colonization in India, which [would] most certainly and rapidly lead to the dissolution of our Indian empire."[85] The American Revolution was one of the major reasons for this concern. Amales Tripathi notes that the governors feared that any settlements would lead to the "colonization of India and her ultimate defection, like the American colonies, from the mother country."[86]

Finally, the longitudinal case of India demonstrates that certain instances of what is normally understood as colonialism constitute only a special case of a more general explanation accounting for the lack of institutionalized money and credit systems. I say "certain instances" because not all cases of colonialism represent the same power asymmetries that are detrimental to the emergence of institutionalized financial systems. This could be the reason why other putatively colonial states, Canada being one example, did develop such systems. Similarly, many ostensibly noncolonial situations, as the case of Mughal India demonstrated, can produce conditions that hinder the emergence of state-connected financial systems. This is not to gainsay the differences between the money and credit system of late precolonial India and the system that emerged later; from a certain perspective, the position of indigenous financial capital holders deteriorated considerably. Yet these differences fall into the same category in the theoretical framework proposed here: in neither case did governing elites need to incorporate networks of capital holders and hence institutionalize their role in the state itself.

APPENDIX 4.1. MUGHAL FINANCES

Abu'l Fazl's *A'in I Akbari* (which was part of the official history of the Mughal Empire under Emperor Akbar, who ruled between 1556 and 1606) contains the best contemporaneous account of Mughal finances, including detailed accounting of revenue sources. The territory was divided into twelve *subas* (provinces), and the only province for which he lists any source other than land revenue is Gujarat, which contained all the major ports of the empire.[87] Fazl estimates port revenues to be only around Rs. 80,000 out of the province's total of Rs. 11,000,000.[88] Fazl probably greatly underestimated both the total revenue and the amount accruing from trade.[89] Indeed, according to M. N. Pearson, who derived his figures from many mutually consistent Persian and Portuguese sources (and not the *A'in*), total revenue from Gujarat "was claimed to be Rs. 57,550,000," of which customs payments (in 1572) constituted Rs. 4,000,000.[90] The figures for Gujarat should, however, be treated with some caution because, as Pearson points out, "it is . . . impossible even to guess how much [total] revenue sea trade produced. A figure here would include land revenue paid on crops destined to be exported, and inland duties paid on these goods, as well as customs duties [which are included in the figures above]." Nonetheless, trade was probably uniquely important to Gujarat relative to the other Mughal provinces, since "Abu'l Fazl gives no figures for the customs revenue of any province of Akbar's empire, except for the incorrect one for Gujarat. Clearly he did not consider it [customs revenue] to be of much importance."[91]

Estimates of the revenues of Bengal in the late seventeenth and early eighteenth centuries (i.e., around the time of Aurangzeb's death) are somewhat more difficult to obtain, but some evidence does exist. According to the seventeenth-century historian Muhammad Sharif Hanafi, the *total* annual revenue of Bengal was 500,000,000 *dams*, or roughly Rs. 12,500,000, during Shah Jahan's reign (1628–1666).[92] This figure seems to be somewhat reliable, since another contemporary historian, Bakhtawar Khan, puts the figure at about Rs. 13,000,000 during Aurangzeb's time, presumably in the last third of the seventeenth century.[93] We also know from various documents that the land revenue assessment of Bengal in 1700 was Rs. 11,728,541.[94] So revenues from sources other than land rent appear to be minuscule.

APPENDIX 4.2. EAST INDIA COMPANY FINANCES, 1757–1837

It is difficult to find a complete accounting of EIC finances prior to about 1835: the available evidence is somewhat fragmentary. Yet that partial picture is consistent with the more complete figures for revenue and debt (which functions as an indirect and approximate measure of total expense) available for later years. Governor General John Shore reported that while land revenue receipts amounted to between Rs. 31,000,000 and 33,000,000 (£3,000,000–£4,000,000) between 1791 and 1793, the salt monopoly accounted for between Rs. 8,000,000 (£800,000–£1,000,000) and 11,000,000 (£1,100,000–£2,700,000) during the same time, and the amounts from the opium monopoly were Rs. 2,800,000–2,900,000.[95] Dutch merchants trading in Bengal estimated that in the 1770s the EIC spent £1,000,000 each year over Bengal's annual revenue, which stood at around £4,000,000.[96] H. V. Bowen states that the total Bengal revenue between 1766 and 1781 was almost £38,000,000, an average of almost £2,300,000 per annum.[97] According to Tripathi, the surplus (i.e., after interest payments on debt) from Bengal land revenues in the seventeen years between 1785 and 1802 came to £29,315,979, constituting almost all the Company's land revenue during this period.[98] Land revenue probably went up as the Company added territories in Deccan and North India, in the first decade of the nineteenth century, and all of the erstwhile Maratha territories in 1817.

The rate of interest on EIC debt varied between 8 and 10 percent per annum. If the Dutch estimates are to be believed (and if it is assumed that all the excess spending was covered by debt issues), total Company debt in the 1770s was probably around £9,000,000. Bowen reports that between 1769 and 1772, the EIC borrowed £5,500,000 from the Bank of England; in 1785 it further raised £4,180,000 from the London market, and between 1798 and 1803 it raised over

£6,000,000 again.[99] And between 1808 and 1809, £3,000,000 of India debt was transferred to England. The Company met the payment of these bills of exchange by raising its bond debts in London—with parliamentary authorization—or through direct payments by the British government "toward its account with the Company."[100] Again in 1812, the Company raised another £2,000,000 in London toward India debt payments.[101] Marshall estimates that in the early nineteenth century, the Company's obligations in London alone (e.g., interest, dividend to shareholders, pensions) amounted to about £3,000,000 a year.[102] Between 1756 and 1834 the Company's total *payments* in London toward debts incurred in India and bills of exchange (the two were not mutually exclusive, since sometimes debts in India were secured in exchange for bills in London, and other times the debts or a portion thereof were directly payable in London) amounted to £67,631,634.[103]

Banks and the State

The United States, 1790–1836

An Overview

THE HISTORY OF BANKING AND CREDIT (and their regulation) in the United States in the early nineteenth century presents instructive opportunities for observing and interrogating the modalities of institutional origins and development. Given the almost complete absence of financial institutions and instruments prior to independence, the period between the establishment of the first banks and the proliferation of banking as an activity (and hence the creation of a money market) allows one to carefully examine the factors that affected the contours of that market soon after its inception. For instance, what accounted for the progressive lowering of entry barriers to banking and hence the relatively rapid expansion of banks in the United States? Why did the federal government not assume a more active role in banking regulation? And finally, what led to the rise and demise of the two institutions that came closest to being federal government banks?

The questions raised above can be taken, more generally, as interrogating an already institutionalized money and credit system. Though the individual inquiries have been addressed in various ways, sometimes indirectly, by historians and political scientists, the objective of this chapter is to put them in a single theoretical framework (as sketched out in Chapters 1 and 2), while responding to some of the extant discussion.

The broad details the questions refer to are familiar to scholars: the establishment of the Bank of North America and then the first Bank of the United States; the controversies—legal and political—in the aftermath of its creation; the rapid proliferation of state-chartered banks; the failure of the Bank to secure a charter renewal; the establishment of the second Bank of the United States in the aftermath of the War of 1812; President Jackson's distaste for that Bank and the ensuing "bank war" between its supporters and opponents; and, finally, Jackson's decision to veto the renewal of the second Bank's charter. These events have been interpreted as either contestations over ideas and public philosophies or squabbles over economic self-interests.[1] Furthermore, the particular economic interests instrumental to these developments have been variously conceptualized as those of small farmers, artisans, small or middling businessmen and financiers, and established, large businesses and financiers. To take a couple of examples, while Arthur Schlesinger Jr. attributes Jackson's actions to his populist base, Hammond argues that the downfall of the two Banks was due to opposition from businessmen attached to state banks who demanded cheaper money and resented the control that the two federally chartered banks exerted.[2] This chapter seeks to mediate between these interpretations with the aid of the theoretical framework proposed earlier. Using the language of *necessary* and *sufficient* conditions, I seek to account for the rise and fall of the two Banks of the United States. The chapter asks this: Given all the interests implicated in the literature, which ones can be seen as indispensable to the developments mentioned above? Counterfactually stated, what are the existing factors without which the two Banks of the United States would have survived? I suggest that investor cohesion was a crucial factor explaining these events. The downfall of both the Banks and the consequent lowering of barriers to entry can be attributed to the inability of investors as a group to agree and act on their common preferences. Further, this inability *could* be a direct consequence of the strategic actions of the executive of the state (in this case, the president). A recapitulation of part of the theoretical framework should help clarify this proposition.

As Chapters 1 and 2 noted, understanding the origins of the credible institutional commitment that enabled the emergence of modern credit and banking systems also helps in understanding subsequent changes to the systems. This is because credible commitments institutionalize the preferences of certain well-defined groups as well as their bargaining power; in the case of the United States, the commitment institutionalized preferences that were common to all financial capital holders *qua* investors. In doing so it delimited certain paths of change, or at least made them more unlikely. Yet, almost as a corollary, it also enabled changes in other directions.

Once the foundations for institutionalized cooperation between rulers and capital holders were established, further developments (that is, given those foundations, or "basic" institutions that represented the common preferences and power of investors) would depend on the relative bargaining powers of rulers and capital holders and hence the ability of capital holders to unite and undertake collective action. As I argued in Chapter 2, rulers tend to have an institutional advantage in this regard by virtue of their ability to propose policies that could have a differential impact on different groups of investors: for instance, policies that reward some groups of investors at others' expense. However, this advantage would be crucially contingent on rulers not disturbing the institutional status quo serving some of the fundamental interests of capital holders as a class. Moreover, as Chapter 2 explained, this aspect of the argument is consistent with Thomas Ferguson's claim—in his "investment theory" of competition between political parties—that there would be no competition over issues that involved the "vital interests of all major investors."[3] The theoretical framework I propose in this book is somewhat more specific in that it precisely identifies the institutional sources of those "vital interests."

As I demonstrate below, fundamental institutions that were a part of the credible commitment between governing elites and financial capital holders represented the "vital interests of all major investors." These institutions were fundamental or vital in the sense that they served the interests of all investors while at the same time empowering them as a group so that they were in a position, by virtue of the institutional bargain, to inflict an unacceptable cost on the state in case of any deviation from the compact. Preexisting basic institutions restricted the scope of further institutional change in certain directions precisely because these institutions empowered a set of actors that had both the incentive and the ability to defend the institutional status quo. This chapter demonstrates the plausibility of the counterfactual to the unity (and hence noncompetition) of investors over vital institutional interests by showing that investors in general opposed policy proposals that threatened these interests irrespective of their (divergent) positions on other issues that were not vital. Consequently, vital institutional interests never became the subject of open political contestation.[4]

Given the existence of vital interests (that became embodied in institutions), this chapter also examines conditions under which the interests of investors diverged and thus produced political competition. These conflicts meant that other paths of change that did not threaten vital institutions were still open. Such paths created opportunities for certain privileged institutional actors—as we shall see, one of these actors was the executive of the state itself—to propose policies designed to affect different groups of investors in different ways, preventing collective action by dividing them. The bargaining power of investors vis-à-vis the executive of the state varied by institutional setting: investors were considerably weaker, and rulers or executives relatively stronger, within domains that did not include vital institutions.[5]

Thus, examining alternative historical hypotheses in light of the available evidence, I argue that the degree of cohesion among financial capital holders explains the developments mentioned above.[6] Specifically, the degree of cohesion was a *necessary* condition explaining these developments, and the degree of cohesion itself was *sufficiently* (though not *necessarily*) a function of executive action. To demonstrate the *necessity* of the degree of cohesion among investors for developments in the money market, this chapter argues that the downfall of the first Bank of the United States can be traced directly to divisions among financial capital holders. To show that executive action was *sufficient* to affect investor cohesion, it argues that the demise of the second Bank of the United States and the accompanying changes in the money market can be traced directly to the actions of the executive in successfully creating divisions among investors. What is particularly notable—because it makes this explicit—is that the president succeeded in doing so even after supporters of the Bank had managed to create a consensus among investors in its favor.[7] This is a powerful illustration of the *contextually* privileged institutional position of the executive of the state vis-à-vis investors: the executive's ability to create schisms among capital holders was crucially predicated on conformity with certain vital preexisting institutional arrangements, so any challenge to these arrangements would have not only united wealth holders but also gone against the interests of the state itself.

Other scholars have interpreted and explained the events above in somewhat different ways. As discussed in Chapter 2, one line of thought points to the crucial role of ideology, or the public philosophy of policy makers.[8] My argument here does not gainsay the role of ideology; indeed, it can accommodate the ideology or public philosophy of policy makers without any inconsistency. Although ideas and public philosophies can provide links or road maps between means and ends, the prominence of particular philosophies and their specific interpretations in policy terms depend on power dynamics and hence also the institutions that are the sources of bargaining advantage. This suggests that agents would support the ideas or philosophies that could be expected to lead to the closest approximation of the ends— both economically self-interested and otherwise—that they value.[9]

For instance, an examination of these events demonstrates that even though philosophies and ideas cannot be reduced to pure gain seeking, economic actors often espoused ideologies that prescribed actions or measures that could be predicted to favor their interests. Those not motivated by egoistic gain had to reckon with groups motivated by such interests, whose bargaining power was directly attributable to the institutional context. This is precisely the reason why even an institutionally advantaged actor, such as the president—who, as I demonstrate, was not acting at the behest of any gain-seeking group—could not attain the policy goals that would otherwise seem to be most proximate to his ideology.

The Money Market and the State, 1790–1836

Chapter 3 accounted for the basis of the vital interests shared by all investors. It was the institutional compact forming the basis of the U.S. financial system, also enshrined in the Constitution, that gave financial investors *as a class* an interest in defending, and the means to defend, very specific and identifiable aspects of the institutional features of the state. The compact, in turn, was a direct outcome of the Revolutionary War, which necessitated cooperation between the incipient governing or state elites and financial investors. The federal Constitution prohibited all currency issuances by state assemblies, thus excluding all but those who had the willingness and ability to form chartered institutions called commercial banks from having a direct influence on the total stock of payment medium in the economy. This restriction was clearly in the interest of all potential or actual financial capital holders, since it considerably attenuated the legislature's ability to diminish or repudiate debt. Federal assumption of all outstanding debts created a market in government securities, which in turn created a mutually beneficial institutional structure between the state and private investors, including banks. That was also why Hamilton opposed any moves that would give the legislature control over a national bank.

This, then, was the fundamental pact that undergirded the financial system of the newly formed United States. Any challenge to this compact would have been against the interests of every financial capital holder, and, consequently, this institutional arrangement also defined the limits of further policy changes. In fact, the fundamental institutional compact accounts for why changes in certain other directions, though entertained, did not eventually come to pass, thus illustrating both the counterfactual possibilities and their theoretical improbability.

Once an institutionalized financial system was established in the United States, even the policy makers most hostile to banking realized that as long as the state had to depend on resources controlled by merchants and bankers, banks were here to stay. On the other hand, merchants and businessmen shared certain policy preferences that were clearly consistent with their common interest: the perpetuation of banking institutions and the recognition of all banknotes by the government. Thus, consensus on these issues was likely to be easily attained relative to others that were less obvious or whose implications were less clear. Rulers therefore were likely to have an advantage in any dispute not involving the basic issues discussed above. They could hope to exploit or create dissensions within groups of financial capital holders, but only within certain parameters—namely, as long as they did not threaten the fundamental aspects of the financial system by withdrawing support from all banking institutions, such as by derecognizing banknotes or by establishing government banks fully under legislative control. In other words, institutional positioning gave the executive of the state greater bargaining power vis-à-vis subgroups of bankers under circumstances where issues did not involve investors' vital interests.

Since bankers and financiers could not necessarily be expected to agree on policy preferences beyond those described above, a change in the status quo could be initiated by significant subgroups of financial capital holders if they expected to gain from the change. I argue below that this was the case with the first Bank's failure to gain an extension of its charter. Changes in status quo could, however, also be initiated by the executive of the state, and as long as they were within the parameters mentioned above, they could be supported by subgroups of capital holders that expected to gain from such changes (if these subgroups were large enough). This meant that the executive could successfully create situations in which the relationship between particular groups of financial capital holders became a zero-sum situation: policies that rewarded one subgroup directly at the expense of the other made it extremely difficult for the subgroups to form a unified front. In this way the executive could create dissension even where consensus over the status quo existed among capital holders, and this is precisely what happened with President Jackson's refusal to recharter the Bank of the United States. Both cases reveal attempts by variously interested groups and individuals to promote cohesion or dissension among investors, illustrating the deployment of ideas, ideologies, and public philosophies for specified policy ends.

The Demise of the First Bank of the United States

As Hamilton indicated, the Bank of the United States was created as a private bank (even though the government initially owned 20 percent of its total capital). Hamilton clearly wanted to preclude the possibility of governments establishing and directing their own banks. If established in large enough numbers or with large enough capital, publicly owned banks, responsible to legislators, could have circumvented the prohibition on currency issuances by governments, if and when under the influence of nonmercantile groups.[10] In this sense the Bank was a private bank that had an unfair (from certain ideological perspectives) advantage over other such banks due to its close relationship with the federal government. The government deposited the bulk of its revenue with the first Bank and therefore would not have allowed it to fail or suffer great losses.[11] The fact that the Bank lent to the federal government was therefore a long-term insurance of sorts, and this insurance policy was available to only the first Bank. This simple fact, obvious to many, made it very easy for divisions to emerge in the ranks of major investors.

Yet at the time of its founding, there was substantial consensus among financial capital holders on the status of the Bank of the United States. Existing banks were generally supportive, since most of them had been, in Redlich's words, "set up more or less under the influence of the Bank of North America," the predecessor to the first Bank.[12] Indeed, even prior to the founding of the Bank of the United States, there was considerable cooperation among the founders of early banks. As Redlich puts it, this was natural, "since they had worked hand in hand during the Revolutionary War and were bound together, if not by family ties and friendship, then at least by the same political creed and identical interests within society and the body politic."[13] It was therefore not surprising that upon the creation of the Bank of the United States, "the Bank of New York and the Massachusetts Bank acted as its agents to receive local subscriptions, and the Bank of North America welcomed it in the friendliest spirit."[14]

Further unity among merchants and investors in various cities of the United States was aided by an active movement to acquire shares in the Bank. The establishment of branches in various parts of the country was aimed at reinforcing this objective. As James Wettereau notes, "The wide distribution of its membership [i.e., stockholding] testified equally to the desire to have the popularity of the institution serve as '*cement of the Union*' and the wish to secure the prompt organization of branches."[15] As for the other banks, Hamilton believed that the interests of the first Bank were not contrary to theirs.[16] Indeed, he actively tried to promote friendly cooperation between the existing banks and the Bank of the United States.[17]

Yet others were not sanguine about the stability of this consensus. Boston merchant Fisher Ames was particularly prescient in his prediction that state banks would narrow the business of the Bank of the United States "and may become dangerous instruments in the hands of state partizans [*sic*] who may have bad points to carry." He therefore opined, "All the influence of the monied men ought to be wrap'd up in the union and in one Bank."[18] That Ames was to be proved correct was often revealed during times of crisis: the Bank's enormous capital relative to other banks gave it considerable influence in the money market, which was felt most acutely in such times.[19] A second difficulty in maintaining long-term coherence concerned the customer base of the respective banks, which, in turn, was evidence of the increasing diversification—in terms of both size and kinds of business activities—of the emerging U.S. business community.

Thus, demands for new banks often accompanied allegations of credit discrimination by the established banks. For example, in 1804, newspapers reported that the Pennsylvania assembly heard demands for chartering a new bank called Philadelphia Bank, whose promoters alleged that the other Philadelphia banks, including the Bank of the United States, favored particular political inclinations and that creditworthy people with other opinions were excluded from credit.[20]

The reasons cited for the demand for a new bank go beyond the particular case in question and are illustrative of the larger difficulties of maintaining some sort of consensus among investors and bankers when it came to money market–related policies. Established banks often practiced credit discrimination, though it is not clear whether this was for partisan reasons, independent of other typically economic reasons such as differences in clientele. Naomi Lamoreaux's research on nineteenth-century U.S. banking demonstrates that at least in early nineteenth-century New England, banks often acted more like "investment clubs," restricting their lending activities to only designated groups of "insiders."[21] Lamoreaux contends that one important reason for "insider lending" was risk reduction by banks. Since "insiders" were often linked by familial or kinship ties, this signaled creditworthiness.[22] Yet it is not difficult to imagine partisan allegiances serving the same function, especially since many "reputable" merchants "were federalists almost by necessity."[23]

It is also probable, though, that creditworthiness was in the eye of the beholder, since, as Redlich puts it, "original banks in some places because of their truly mercantile capital may not have . . . considered smaller merchants, such as shopkeepers, worthy of credit."[24] Credit restriction of this kind could have coincided with partisan splits within the business community, especially as emerging domestically oriented manufacturers started demanding easier credit toward the end of the first decade of the nineteenth century.[25] Even a study that questions the applicability of Lamoreaux's findings to Pennsylvania and New York finds evidence of credit rationing in Pennsylvania that adversely affected "artisans, mechanics, retailers, and lesser merchants [who] found themselves increasingly less able to obtain discounts as larger merchants with more collateral received [an] increasing percentage of loanable funds."[26]

An early indication of dissatisfaction among some financiers is evidenced in an 1804 article by Samuel Blodget, an acquaintance of Thomas Jefferson and a prominent merchant. In an article in the local Democratic Republican newspaper, Blodget articulates the business case against high entry barriers to banking, and also against the first Bank.[27] Ostensibly a defense of a somewhat controversial new bank in the District of Columbia (the Bank of Potomac), the article went far beyond the immediate issue to reveal tensions within the banking and finance community. What is important about this response is that Blodget was defending the new bank not against agrarian or other populist attacks but against fellow bankers and creditors. Blodget accused the established bankers of Massachusetts of opposing new banks, such as his personal projects, in order to earn high interest rates. He further accused them of doing so by influencing state governments.

His criticism of the first Bank followed the same logic: he held up the Bank as an example of a recipient of unfair protection, since it had an exclusive charter from the federal government. He seemed to think that Congress would not renew the Bank's charter once it expired but rather would extend the same privileges accorded to it to all banks thereafter. Further, he argued that there should be little restriction to banking in the United States, since the country had only about $30,000,000 in banking capital while "England alone has . . . above 600,000,000 of dollars of banking capital." Therefore, "to equal her beneficial experience, we might for six millions of people if more compactly situated, carry our banking capital to at least seven times its present sum, and to the same advantage."[28]

That Blodget could not have been the only banker holding these views is evident from his own testimony that despite opposition from the quarters described above, he managed, with the help of sympathetic bankers and financiers, to establish a few banks and an insurance company. The article presaged the splits within the business community as the expiration date of the Bank's charter drew near.

The volume of articles about the Bank increased in the aftermath of a petition presented by stockholders to the Senate in 1808 requesting an extension of the charter for an additional twenty years.[29] The administration was generally in favor of renewal. Secretary of the Treasury Albert Gallatin's March 1809 report to the Senate on the Bank broadly supported renewal.[30] This was especially notable coming from a close confidant of Jefferson. Apparently even James Madison—the incoming president, and the Bank's sometime opponent—was not strongly opposed to the Bank, perhaps due to Gallatin's support for it.[31]

Predictably, Gallatin's report provoked a flurry of articles both in favor of and against the Bank, and these are instructive in understanding both sides' efforts to frame the debate in terms that would influence the reading public. One striking feature of the various articles against the Bank is that in addition to pointing out its ostensible sins and making the usual point that it was unjust for one bank to be privileged over all others, the vast majority of them aimed at convincing merchants and bankers at large that the interests of the Bank were distinct from and independent of the interests of the banking system in general.[32] Abolishing its privileged position in the money market, they argued, would therefore not adversely affect the system and, indeed, could have salutary effects. This suggests that those writing against the Bank were generally careful not to raise criticisms that could unite the banking and business community. Conversely, articles defending the Bank, in addition to replying to the accusers' charges, also argued that failure to recharter it would be deleterious to the system as a whole.

The Bank's defenders argued that given its capitalization and circulation, and since many banks and businesses alike were consequently debtors to the Bank of the United States, denial of a second charter would result in economic catastrophe. Denial would force the Bank to call in its debts, curtail discounts, and drastically reduce circulation. This, in turn, would lead debtor banks to call in their debts—since they could not be expected to possess enough specie in their vaults to meet all their obligations—which would seriously harm even entrepreneurs and businesses that were not directly indebted to the first Bank. This would amount to a systemic crisis. The article "Desultory Reflections," addressed to Congress by Philadelphia businessman and journalist Mathew Carey, made this argument most effectively and was reprinted and cited in Federalist newspapers throughout the country.[33] In addition to the dire consequences alluded to above, Carey pointed out the beneficial role of the Bank as a lender of last resort to other banks. Other somewhat conservative newspapers like the Philadelphia-based *Poulson's American Daily Advertiser* carried articles making similar arguments.[34]

Critics of the Bank responded by pointing out that state banks could easily take over its functions and that the dire prognostications of the defenders were attempts at casting the possible predicament of the Bank's stockholders and debtors—a privileged group—as a general economic problem that would affect every citizen.[35] Thus, the Philadelphia newspaper *Weekly Aurora* published a letter "from a commercial capitalist of New York" that decried the influence of the first Bank over all other New York banks (again, on account of its superior capitalization and government deposits) and hence wished for its demise. This was ostensibly to demonstrate that the first Bank's existence was not necessarily in the interests of all businessmen.[36] Other articles contended that the possible harmful consequences of the failure to recharter the Bank were actually an argument against its continued existence. No single institution that could put the economy in danger or hold the economy hostage should be allowed to exist.[37] Further, any temporary problems due to the cessation of the first Bank's business could be easily addressed by short-term government intervention or by the Bank itself as it wound down its business gradually.[38]

Despite the disingenuousness of many of the arguments against the first Bank, critics were correct that its interests could not be equated with the interests of the money and credit market. Indeed, even Gallatin did not base his defense of the Bank on those grounds. Moreover, he knew that—notwithstanding temporary problems—other banks would be only too happy to receive government deposits and take over the functions of the Bank of the United States. Any bank that received government deposits would have the same insurance policy that the Bank of the United States had. Gallatin was also aware that members of Congress like Jacob Crowninshield of Massachusetts had been arguing that their favored institutions—in Crowninshield's case the Manhattan Company—should be allowed to assist the government instead of the first Bank.[39] Some Federalist newspapers had also accused opponents of the first Bank of being men "who are in hopes of creating some new monied institution, in which they may speculate deeply; or by individuals concerned in some state institution, who may wish to get the government deposits to prop up the credit of some town or country bank in which they or some of their friends are interested."[40]

Gallatin's strongest argument in favor of the Bank was that while the exclusive charter of the Bank of the United States allowed for government oversight of its activities, this would not be the case if deposits were transferred to other banks without such a charter. The government's leverage over banks would then be limited to the threat of withdrawing its deposits.[41] Gallatin's report echoed some arguments that two other earlier petitions—one from the directors of the Bank of the United States and another from Bank stockholders who were also members of the Philadelphia Chamber of Commerce—had made in favor of the Bank.[42]

The only other bank that submitted a petition to Congress in favor of the Bank of the United States was the Bank of New York, which, as noted above, had a fairly good working relationship with it.[43] The four other Philadelphia banks were also reportedly in favor of charter renewal, though they did not present any petitions to Congress.[44] On the other hand, the Bank also had very wealthy opponents. New York businessman John Jacob Astor "sent a verbal message to Gallatin assuring him that if renewal was refused, all his funds and those of his friends to the amount of $2,000,000 would be at the command of the Government . . . in any way that would prevent distress arising from dissolution."[45] Another notable opponent was Senator Samuel Smith of Maryland, who was also "a director of the state bank in Baltimore."[46]

The result was that the vote in Congress that ended the Bank by indefinitely postponing consideration of the renewal bill was very close. George Clinton cast the tie-breaking vote against the Bank in the Senate (tied at 17–17) after the House voted 65–64 in favor of postponement. Democratic Republicans held 27 of the 34 seats in the Senate and 92 of the 142 seats in the House. In the Senate, every member voting against the Bank was a Democratic Republican, but ten Democratic Republicans voted against postponement. Similarly every vote in favor of postponement in the House came from Democratic Republicans, but twenty-one Democratic Republicans also voted against the motion.[47] Some of those voting against were notable agrarians such as Senator John Taylor of South Carolina, Senator John Pope of Kentucky, and Representative Samuel McKee of Kentucky. In the aftermath of the vote, a Hudson-based New York newspaper noted: "The representatives from the important commercial cities of N. York, Philadelphia, Baltimore, Norfolk, and Charleston, including the two largest cities in the Union, voted *against* the bank of the United States. So far as this . . . goes, it at least proves the bank is not that essential prop to commerce which it has been represented to be."[48]

This demonstrates that the business and banking community was clearly divided, confirming Hammond's analysis of the divisions on that question and the effects of those divisions on the eventual vote. Yet this does not sufficiently establish the *necessity* of divisions in the business and credit community for the policy outcome examined here. One way to do that would be to demonstrate that issues on which such a split did not exist did not even progress to any kind of policy agenda. Fortunately, this particular case presents a nice approximation of a controlled experiment that strongly demonstrates the plausibility of the counterfactual that in the absence of divisions among investors, the charter would have been renewed.

Two oft-cited criticisms of the Bank of the United States were that foreigners owned most of the stocks and that the Bank unfairly privileged a relatively small set of stockholders and bankers over others. There were two other less often reported positions articulated by agrarians and other Democratic Republicans. The first was an abiding hostility to all banks.[49] The second position was that banks should not be owned or "managed by individuals interested only in their private capacity" and that therefore banks ought to be owned and operated either by state governments or jointly by the federal and state governments.[50] It is easy to see why the latter position would have seemed attractive to agrarians and advocates of more radical forms of democracy. A bank owned and run by the government would allow the relatively numerous parts of the voting population to have a lot of input in monetary policy.[51] For the same reason, it would be unacceptable to all merchants and bankers—including those who otherwise opposed the Bank of the United States. In this case we have very clear evidence that the possibility of establishing a bank jointly run by state and federal governments was officially suggested and, as the theoretical framework would predict, failed to make any headway.

Gallatin's first report did not support the Bank of the United States unqualifiedly. He was well aware of the strongest criticisms of the Bank and sought to respond to them in the report, which suggested changes to the new charter that addressed almost all of the most powerful challenges. His changes, if carried out, would have resulted in a different kind of a national bank—in some respects a true national bank—that would have been a radical departure from the status quo. In the last part of the report, Gallatin proposed a plan to address concerns over the issue of foreign stock ownership and the unfair privilege of Bank stockholders. He suggested that the new charter could increase the capital of the Bank to $30,000,000 and that the total stock could be shared among individuals ($5,000,000), state governments ($15,000,000), and the federal government (the remainder). Moreover, management and direction of the new bank were to be shared between the stockholding parties.[52] This would mean that foreigners would no longer hold stocks of the new Bank and it could no longer be accused of functioning solely for the benefit of a small group.

The problem, of course, was that the suggested charter would have jeopardized the original pact with bankers and merchants as a group. It could have allowed nonbankers and nonmerchants to have considerable input into decisions about the total stock of the payment medium in the economy, and this was unacceptable to not only the stockholders and directors of the Bank but all existing bankers and creditors, irrespective of their position on the rechartering question.

The reaction in the Federalist newspapers to Gallatin's alternative plan was therefore predictable. While they lauded Gallatin for defending the existing Bank, they chided him for his suggestions. The plan, they said, would unduly politicize finance and reduce "confidence."[53] Some portrayed the new plan as more conducive to the development of an "aristocracy" than the existing Bank was.[54] While the Democratic Republican papers were largely silent about the alternative plan, Duane's *Aurora*, which was at the forefront of the battle against the first Bank, also criticized Gallatin's alternative plan even though it addressed some of the criticisms that the *Aurora* had been carrying.[55]

As it happened, a bill containing Gallatin's plan was referred to a committee chaired by the Federalist senator from Delaware, James Bayard. However, the bill did not proceed any further: discussion on it was postponed by a motion from Bayard.[56] Finally, as Hammond has noted, some agrarian members voting against indefinite postponement had accurately realized that failure to recharter the Bank would not affect most of the other state banks, and they foresaw the probable implications of the absence of a nationally chartered bank. No friends of banks, these politicians found the Bank of the United States with its regional branches preferable to a plethora of state banks, none of which could even be brought under government oversight. In the words of Representative McKee of Kentucky, "You have all the evils of the United States Bank without any of the advantages."[57]

The banks selected to take over federal deposits from the Bank of the United States constitute an interesting, though predictable, list. Among them were the Bank of Baltimore (with which Senator Smith was connected) and the Manhattan Company (Crowninshield's favored bank). Others were the Union and Massachusetts Banks in Boston, the Mechanics' Bank in New York, the Bank of Pennsylvania and the Farmers' and Mechanics' Bank in Philadelphia, the Commercial and Farmers' Bank in Baltimore, the Norfolk branch of the Bank of Virginia, the State Bank in Charleston, and the Bank of New Orleans.[58] All of the banks were selected to replace the branches of the Bank of the United States in the same cities, although there was no replacement provided for the branch in Savannah. Additionally the banks that already had government deposits continued to keep them. Thus, despite some temporary difficulties, even some Philadelphia banks that were reportedly uneasy with the failure of rechartering gained at the expense of the Bank of the United States.

As the case of the first Bank demonstrates, any policy move that did not challenge basic institutional arrangements could have different distributional consequences for different investor groups. Under such circumstances, it would be very difficult for capital holders to present a united front. It was therefore easy to imagine a situation where institutionally advantaged policy makers could, if they were able to attract a large enough subset or group of investors and capital holders, enact their favored policies. Even where divisions among investors did not arise spontaneously, government leaders could propose policies that met their own preferences while also entailing differential distributive consequences for a large enough group of capital holders to secure their support or acquiescence. This was precisely the case in the dechartering of the second Bank of the United States.

Executive Action and (the Fall of) the Second Bank of the United States

The second Bank of the United States was established after a particularly tumultuous period. The War of 1812 had stretched federal government finances and directly resulted in the country's first bank suspension of specie payments as British troops invaded Washington, D.C., in the summer of 1814. In contrast to the first Bank, the second was created at the initiative of financial investors close to the Democratic Republican Party, such as John Jacob Astor, Stephen Girard, and David Parish, who held substantial government debt, which at that time was trading at deep discount. To summarize very briefly, the Bank's establishment entailed recreating the consensus among investors that had been fractured to cause the downfall of the first Bank of the United States. This, in turn, entailed constructing a bank whose distributional consequences would be acceptable not only to government bond holders such as Astor and Girard but also to (mostly Federalist) financiers hostile to the government in power. This eventually succeeded with the establishment of a bank—the second Bank of the United States—that managed to generally satisfy all the major parties to the negotiation: dissident Federalist financiers, financiers close to the government, and the government itself.[59]

Without going into all the details of the negotiations over the charter of the bank, it would be useful here to point out some of the principal features that succeeded in satisfying all three groups. First, holders of government securities were allowed to exchange their holdings for bank stock; second, the bank could suspend specie payments only when authorized by Congress (in others words, the president of the United States could not unilaterally do so); third, the government would appoint five of the twenty-five directors of the bank, but the president of the bank was to be elected by stockholders; and fourth, the government's subscription to the bank (which was to be a fifth of the total) was to be paid in specie (one-quarter) and government bonds (three-quarters). While the first provision was clearly aimed at satisfying government bond holders, the second, third, and the fourth emerged as dissident financiers, who were not otherwise opposed to a bank, sought to ensure that the government did not have too many direct levers of influence over the money market, while the government sought to extract some amount of control over the bank in return for a charter. A quick perusal of all the alternative proposals that failed, as well as the provisions added or removed when at least one of the three groups was dissatisfied, supports this conclusion.[60]

Intra-investor and government negotiations notwithstanding, a brief analysis of the fate of one of the alternative proposals attests to the general awareness among key policy makers that adherence to the basic or vital interests of investors (as a class) was necessary for the success of any institutional plan. There were agrarians such as John Eppes, a Virginia congressman and Jefferson's son-in-law, who did not think that a bank was necessary.[61] He was an influential member of the Ways and Means Committee who believed, along with some other agrarians, that in order to provide a uniform medium of exchange, the government should issue treasury bills, which could become the currency of the nation. Such a possibility was clearly unacceptable to all bankers, since it would put the government, which in Hamilton's words was "liable to being too much influenced by public necessity," in charge. This was, indeed, what Secretary of the Treasury Alexander J. Dallas replied when Eppes formally asked him to comment on the idea. Echoing Hamilton, Dallas stated that such a policy would "excite general dissatisfaction among the present holders of public debt and, generally, distrust among capitalists, who are accustomed to advance their money to the Government," thus dealing a blow to government credit.[62]

The importance of intra-investor consensus to the establishment and functioning of the Bank was therefore not lost on its contemporaries. Dallas sought to reassure state banks and their stockholders that although the new bank would be a competitor, "competition does not imply hostility." In a manifestly transparent appeal to the common class interests of all bankers and financiers, he elaborated:

> The commercial interests, and the personal association of stockholders, will generally be the same, in the State banks and in the National Bank. *The directors of both institutions will naturally be taken from the same class of citizens*; and experience has shown, not only the policy, but the existence of those sympathies, by which the intercourse of a National Bank and the State banks has been, and always ought to be, regulated, for their common credit and security.[63]

Yet as the demise of the Bank twenty years later would demonstrate, the state could easily create divisions in some circumstances.

It is worth highlighting here the role of Jackson's ideology or philosophy in his decision to veto the act renewing the charter of the second Bank of the United States. As I noted earlier, he was not acting at the behest of any subgroup of investors or, indeed, that of workers, farmers, or any other noninvestor group. As Susan Hoffmann points out, "Jackson was . . . not responding to popular demand to dismantle the bank," since "there was . . . widespread support for the institution throughout the country: by state legislatures, by state banks, and among the people generally."[64] Indeed, there is very little evidence—at least from an investigation of newspapers between 1825 and 1829—that the legitimacy of the Bank was an issue before Jackson explicitly raised it.[65] Furthermore, an examination of petitions to Congress shows that for every petition opposing the second Bank of the United States, there were roughly four supporting it.[66] This appeared to be the case even among the constituency most favorable to Jackson. Independent artisans and workers' groups, whom Jackson claimed to represent, nonetheless perceived the second Bank as better than the numerous state banks and often said so in their petitions in favor of the Bank.[67] Moreover, Martin Van Buren and the "Albany Regency" notwithstanding, the majority of financial investors and bankers were not opposed to the Bank.[68] It was therefore not a surprise when the bill granting a renewal of charter comfortably passed both houses. Thus, clearly, opposition from some quarters of the banking community did not suffice to defeat the second Bank.

Yet identifying Jackson's ideological motivations does not exclude the role of distributional considerations and the strategic environment in explaining the outcomes. Indeed, given knowledge of the president's motivations, it is not possible to explain what transpired without taking into account the strategic environment, including the economic interests of financial investors. Whatever his ultimate ends, there were serious limits to the possibilities of attaining them; more importantly, Jackson's changing pronouncements and actions demonstrate that he realized this.

Reginald C. McGrane's analysis of the correspondence of Nicholas Biddle, president of the second Bank of the United States, supports Hoffmann's view that Jackson's opposition to the institution was primarily ideological.[69] It appears that Biddle believed that the president was opposed to all chartered banks and, moreover, that Jackson planned to replace the Bank of the United States with a fully government-owned national bank.[70] Jackson's public pronouncements only confirmed this belief. In December 1829, he urged Congress to consider whether it was possible to establish a bank founded on the credit of the government to replace the current bank of the United States.[71]

Jackson's plan would have violated the vital institutional interests of financial investors as a class. Both Biddle and opponents of the Bank who were close to Jackson (but *not* opposed to state banks) realized this. In fact, Biddle hoped that Jackson's preferred plan would force detracting financial capital holders to make common cause with the supporters of the Bank.[72] He therefore hoped to convey the message that opponents of the Bank would face an even worse outcome if the charter were not renewed.[73] On the other hand, anti-Bank financiers close to Jackson generally remained silent on his alternative plan, focusing instead on his opposition to the Bank. This dynamic was replicated in Congress: major supporters of the Bank assailed the president's plan while the chief opponents confined their criticism to the existing Bank without commenting on Jackson's alternative proposal. Thus, a committee asked to consider the president's address harshly criticized his plan for a national bank founded on government credit, equating such an institution with despotism, while at the same time defending the current Bank of the United States. The minority report of the same committee, while very critical of the Bank, was completely silent on the president's plan. Indeed, it contended instead that state banks were more than equipped to take over the function of the Bank of the United States.[74]

In his second address, Jackson restated his plan for a fully government-owned bank, which would be a branch of the Treasury. However, this time, sensing opposition from state banks and other financiers close to him, he suggested that the new bank could not issue any paper (thus in effect leaving this exclusively to state banks), though it would accept state bank paper.[75] His reasoning was that this way the new bank could regulate state banks—by forcing them to pay out specie against their own (deposit or payment) notes—without competing with them. Jackson was soon to realize that this plan had very little congressional support.[76] Thus, in his third address in 1831, he explicitly pronounced that the matter of what should replace the Bank of the United States should be left to Congress.

This history demonstrates that though the president was not acting at the behest of a few anti-Bank financiers and his opposition was, indeed, ideological, he realized the limits of his autonomy insofar as enacting policy was concerned. This is a somewhat different proposition from the one advanced by Hammond. My argument here is that there was a convergence of preferences between anti-Bank financiers and the president over their common opposition to the Bank of the United States. Yet it was Jackson's opposition and his subsequent actions, *not* the opposition of the anti-Bank financiers, that was sufficient to bring about the outcome of interest here. This relationship becomes more evident as we review Jackson's strategic actions in creating wider divisions among financial capital holders.

As was apparent from his changing positions with respect to a replacement for the Bank, Jackson seems to have been quite cognizant of the fact that he could not afford to unite financial capital holders against him. On the other hand the Bank's president, Biddle, was hoping precisely for such an outcome. Indeed, he commented that the president's note following the veto was reminiscent of revolutionaries like [Maximilien] Robespierre and [Jean-Paul] Marat, and therefore had the potential to unite all bankers and financiers against him.[77] Despite Jackson's reelection following the veto, it was quite probable that the Bank would be able to obtain a charter renewal. Since the charter was to expire in 1836, the Bank still had four more years to secure a renewal from Congress with a veto-proof majority. And this is precisely where fracturing any potential unity among financial capital holders became vital—indeed, *necessary*.

To attain his desired ends, Jackson could not rely on any policy that might solidify cohesion among bankers and financiers. This was clearly demonstrated to him by the lack of support for his alternative plans among investors and policy makers. Whatever Jackson's personal motivations or desires, they had to bend to this strategic situation. One sure way of creating discord was to selectively reward some banks and bankers at the expense of the Bank of the United States, so that the Bank would be forced to resist; this, in turn, would lead to a full-scale conflict between these institutions. The president had the upper hand here in the form of a very potent weapon—namely, the government deposits in the Bank.

It was at this point that Jackson sought to entice other state banks, including what were to be known later as his "pet banks," to hold government deposits.[78] In less than a year he had gone from disapproving of all banking institutions to mounting a defense of state banks against those who contended that government deposits were much safer with the second Bank of the United States. This came out most clearly in Jackson's conflict with his new treasury secretary, William Duane. Like many Jacksonian Democrats, Duane "had always been 'opposed to the United States Bank, and to all such aristocratic monopolies,'" including state banks.[79] Duane had been appointed on the assumption that his antibank views would make him amenable to Jackson's plan to end the Bank. Unfortunately for Jackson, Duane's principled distaste for all chartered banking institutions meant that he was opposed to rewarding a group of state banks—which in his view were less sound and more prone to the tendencies that he disliked among such institutions—at the expense of the Bank of the United States, especially since he perceived, correctly, that the Bank's ensuing credit contraction would probably harm its debtors and possibly cause a panic. Duane therefore refused to carry out the president's orders to transfer deposits from the Bank to the selected state banks. Jackson first tried to convince him that without this transfer, the Bank of the United States would probably succeed in securing a renewed charter by a veto-proof two-thirds majority in Congress.[80] But when these efforts failed, the president promptly dismissed Duane and appointed Roger Taney—who was a confirmed opponent of the Bank but friendly toward state banks—as the secretary of the treasury. Taney finally carried out the order.

This again demonstrates that ideas and ideologies by themselves do not suffice to explain outcomes. Here is an example of the same general public philosophy leading to two very different policy prescriptions: indeed, Jackson's differences with Duane can be explained only with reference to the strategic and institutional situation, of which the president seemed to be fully cognizant. In addition, his rationale for insisting on a speedy transfer of funds to the "pet banks" indicates that he was hoping to achieve some very specific outcomes. His hopes were not in vain.

Congress initially opposed the president's move but could do little beyond censuring him.[81] The government soon began the process of gradually moving its deposits from the Bank of the United States to the designated banks. The "pet banks" took advantage of their position by preemptively demanding deposits from the Bank. The Bank for its part soon began a process of credit contraction, ostensibly in order to reduce its operation in proportion to the loss of public deposits.

Yet, as Ralph C. H. Catterall observes, "The enormous reductions made by the bank were certainly in excess of any possible danger, and were continued long after any such danger threatened." The Bank's strategy was quite transparent: it "hoped to force a re-charter, or at least a restoration of the deposits, by exercising a monetary pressure upon the country."[82] Though it initially seemed to elicit the desired response among businessmen who blamed the government for its actions in removing deposits, the Bank finally began "steadily losing friends" as the distress persisted.[83] The reasons were easy to understand. As long as monetary distress lasted only a short while, the Bank could hope to mobilize opinion in its favor by demonstrating the president's culpability. But "if pressure went so far as to ruin merchants, it would alienate that class and convince the people that the bank was at fault; if it was continued while all around failures were daily occurring, the people would be persuaded that the bank was too powerful and therefore dangerous."[84]

By 1834, the Bank's erstwhile allies were growing highly critical of its actions. Even Gallatin, hitherto one of the Bank's staunchest defenders, spoke out harshly against it.[85] By the end of 1834, there was so much anger against the Bank that Biddle had to send his wife and child away from Philadelphia and surround his home with armed guards during the elections that year. The Whig Party, which lost the elections resoundingly, blamed their loss on the public perception that they were too close to the Bank. The election and what came shortly before it decisively sealed its fate.

Jackson's maneuver had thus succeeded. Using his institutional position he had managed to create a zero-sum situation between the

Bank of the United States and other financial investors, most of whom were the Bank's former supporters. Yet he could do this only because of his adherence to certain basic preexisting institutional features of the financial system; the fact that he had to adhere to these features must have become evident as a result of reactions to his initial alternative plans. On the other hand, it also bears reiteration that this interpretation is different from the one that asserts that the president acted at the *behest* of anti-Bank financiers. That Jackson strategically manipulated the situation with some help from anti-Bank financers—assistance that this group was only too happy to provide—in order to attain his own ends would be a more accurate representation of the events that transpired. In fact, although the details are not of immediate importance here, the Jackson administration's subsequent conflicts against the "pet banks" only reinforce this interpretation.[86]

CONCLUDING REMARKS

This chapter demonstrated how and why differences in bargaining power, once institutionalized, are reproduced over generations. Thus, for example, in prohibiting governments from issuing payment media, the Constitution institutionalized the power of financiers and those with the ability to establish private banks. This sector of the economy was now insulated from any *direct* public politics: a political act in itself. Once the financial system was based on these fundamental institutional features, any challenge to them would result in a disruption the entire system of public and private finance. This, in turn, was because financial investors had vital interests that were intimately tied to these institutional features; this implies that, much as Thomas Ferguson has argued, any policy prescription that threatened these interests would not become the basis of formal political contestation. Yet as noted in the literature on historical institutionalism, leaders could enact changes in certain directions using their enhanced bargaining power in other institutional contexts; at the same time, the ability to promote change was predicated on adherence to certain preexisting institutional features.

The chapter also demonstrated that although ideas and public philosophies were closely tied to policy positions and institutional outcomes, there was not a direct correspondence between them. The same general public philosophy was used both in support of and against the two Banks of the United States. Why the same general public philosophy implied different policy positions to different actors becomes intelligible once one examines the surrounding institutional situations and practices, as Krippner has suggested.[87] In order to do so, one is compelled to reckon with the distributional impact of institutions and the role of power in their emergence.

Finally, the demise of the second Bank of the United States was an event of substantial significance in the history of the U.S. financial system because a federal system of banking did not emerge again until after the Civil War. Banking devolved to the states, with the result that barriers to entry were considerably lowered; this transformed the nature of the money market. Indeed, each instance where a national bank failed to gain a renewed charter saw an enormous increase in the rate of establishment of state-chartered banks. As Gallatin noted about fifteen years after the fall of the first Bank, "The creation of new state banks, in order to fill the chasm, was a natural consequence of the dissolution of the Bank of the United States. And, as is usual under such circumstances, the expectation of great profits gave birth to a much greater number than was wanted."[88] Similarly, between late 1833, when deposits were removed from the second Bank, and early 1836, more than two hundred new banks had been chartered. Additionally, total bank liabilities more than doubled, with most of the expansion taking place in the West and the South. So while note circulation in the East "increased by 50 percent during the three years mentioned," the increase was about 100 percent in the West and about 130 percent in the South.[89] The supporters of both Banks, including Gallatin, who noted and approved of the regulatory role of these institutions, had predicted all this. As this chapter has suggested, there were good reasons why the regulatory role of the two Banks did not suffice to legitimize them in many eyes, as was to be the case with central banking institutions several decades later.

6

Conclusion and
Further Implications

MONEY AND CREDIT MARKETS have been implicated in the process of industrialization in the social science literature at least since Joseph Schumpeter elucidated their role in economic development.[1] Scholars such as Alexander Gerschenkron, Rondo Cameron, and Richard Sylla have since then convincingly argued for their importance in the process of industrialization and, more broadly, economic development in the eighteenth and nineteenth centuries.[2] The same researchers have also noted the crucial role of the state in capital accumulation through these institutions.[3] Indeed, as in the case of late precolonial India, relative state indifference—some would say a certain kind of laissez-faire attitude on the part of the state—actually tends to retard the formation of institutionalized money and credit markets. However, this literature has not provided an account of the conditions under which the institutions of capital accumulation were likely to emerge. Thus, though this book does not seek to explain economic development or industrialization, it has proposed a mechanism through which the spread of European capital could have obstructed financial market formation in now developing areas with otherwise considerable concentration of native mercantile capital. Insofar as such markets can then be linked to industrialization, it suggests an additional hypothesis explaining the lack of industrial development during the eighteenth and nineteenth centuries in many now developing regions. The book has also shown how endogenous institutions can subsequently themselves become sources of relative power.

There are two other groups of arguments that relate institutions and colonial legacies to comparative economic growth. The first, known as the "legal origins" argument, contends that the efficiency of financial systems and, ultimately, economic development is crucially contingent on legal codes and traditions. This book has argued that institutions in general cannot be assumed to be exogenous to economic outcomes and thus provided an endogenous explanation for the emergence of financial institutions; therefore, some of the arguments against the exogeneity of institutions made in Chapter 2 should apply equally to the "legal origins" thesis. The remainder of this chapter further extends these arguments to that thesis and the discussion about it. I assert that such arguments are unable—both theoretically and empirically—to demonstrate that legal codes or traditions operate independently of power relationships to bring about outcomes. Accounting for the origins of institutions is vital to any such demonstration. I then consider some implications of the thesis of this book for another argument, most notably made by Daron Acemoglu, Simon Johnson, and James A. Robinson, that causally associates institutions in general—including legacies of colonialism—with long-term economic development.[4] In both cases I emphasize the need to carefully trace causal processes rather than advance explanations based on averaging many cases, especially since averaging risks conflating phenomena that conceptually do not belong together in the context of the particular question being asked.

COLONIAL LEGACIES, INSTITUTIONS, AND ECONOMIC GROWTH

The "Legal Origins" Argument and Its Critics

Efficiency, or the level of development of financial systems, matters— or so the argument goes—because since it concerns such intermediate factors as the ease of securing credit, barriers to entry to the banking sector, stock market capitalization to the GDP (gross domestic product), government ownership of banks, and bank deposits as a percentage of the GDP, it explains eventual economic development.[5] The "legal origins" literature claims that these intermediate factors are causally related to legal traditions. Its argument, in brief, is that legal traditions are autonomous (i.e., they can be seen as independent from the manner in which they are instituted or the causes of their institution) and tend to incentivize and ultimately habituate certain kinds of behavior, which then influence the levels and kinds of economic activity leading to outcomes such as economic development. Thus, for example, in the case of financial markets, these scholars argue that Anglo-American common-law traditions (especially when compared to civil-law traditions) accord better protection to creditors, require higher information disclosure, and as a result contribute directly to the growth of this sector.[6]

It is very important to emphasize here that this legal traditions–based argument is fundamentally what would be called a "cultural" or "ideational" explanation in political science and sociology. This is also precisely why the analytical and explanatory autonomy of legal traditions is crucial. The argument, in other words, is that whatever the reasons for their initial emergence—Rafael La Porta, Florencio Lopez-de-Silanes, and Andrei Shleifer summarize two basic categories of such reasons—once they emerge they take on a life of their own, are transmitted across generations through education and legal rules, and even become available to be "transplanted" to areas other than those of their first origins.[7]

Mark Roe, among others, has pointed out that the causal mechanism posited in the legal origins argument does not really operate in the manner hypothesized. Thus, for example, Roe and Siegel observe that the distinctions between civil and common law, inasmuch as these are used to account for financial outcomes, are vastly overdrawn.[8] Among other problems, much of the financial regulation in common-law countries arises from administrative codes, rather than fiduciary duties directly inscribed in the law.

Further, there is no reason why such regulatory structures could not develop in civil-law countries too, irrespective of their legal origins—and, indeed, they do so quite frequently.[9] In a similar vein, they also point out that it is not true that civil-law nations regulate more than common-law countries, thus impeding markets. It is also not necessarily true that common-law judges, as the argument goes, are more flexible and therefore better able to protect outsider or minority shareholders. Underlying these various criticisms is the more general point that "there's nothing intrinsic to the mechanics of common law that's property respecting, decentralized, and market oriented."[10] Major violations of property rights have occurred under both systems: "some of history's largest state interventions have occurred in common law countries; prior to twentieth-century communism, history's biggest governmental land-grabs occurred in common law, not civil law countries," for instance.[11] Roe and Siegel also observe that the kinds of laws and institutions that nations adopt depend on "internal circumstances," arguing that it is these circumstances and "not their formalist origin classification" that are worth studying.[12] Along similar lines, they observe that even in the case of colonial imposition of legal codes, the objectives of the colonists determined how codes were applied and followed. As they put it, "Britain was running an empire, not spreading its institutions whenever it could."[13]

Thus, the criticisms above imply that codes are epiphenomenal, endogenous, or marginal to other factors. But what might these other factors be? Here, Roe and Siegel tend to group a wide variety of such possible factors under the general rubric of "political economy." For instance, implying that legal origins might be peripheral to other factors, they say, "If the political-economy isn't in place, then good investor-protection institutions, even if built, will degrade" and, again, "Observers who are not participants may see origins as counting, but nowhere as much as other societal forces, such as political economy ones."[14] While not necessarily a problem, the term "political economy," used as a general descriptor, can obscure as well as illuminate: it can obstruct specific meaning when a number of distinct, independent, or even mutually conflicting causal mechanisms or explanations are grouped under the same category. In such a situation, the category "political economy" becomes a catch-all moniker for any explanation that is not derived from the legal origins framework; as such, there are difficulties inherent in generalizing this as a single alternative explanation over a wide variety of cases (as can be done—the problems with the argument notwithstanding—with the legal origins framework, owing to the fact that the latter does precisely consist of one specific argument).

Thus Roe and Siegel use "political economy" to refer to location within trading circuits, weather and soil conditions (arising out of geographic location in space), culture, institutions, the effects of colonialism, the effects of war and invasions and their influence on the preferences of the median voter, the relative influence of economic groups and actors (capital owners, labor unions), the nature of the electoral system, trade openness where this factor can be imagined to be exogenous, and Cold War–era international politics in the context of discussing financial development in countries ranging from the United States, the United Kingdom, Switzerland, Hong Kong, Malaysia, Singapore, and the so-called developed world in general to Cuba and the developing countries of Asia and Latin America.[15] The order of priority of these various factors or how they combine or interact is never made clear: is geographic location causally prior to the influence of labor unions? Can colonial legacies be superseded by wars? How is culture defined, and what would be a better proxy for it than legal origins (since one criticism of the latter seems to be that it is not a particularly good proxy for culture)?

Answers to such questions are complicated by the fact that the factors or combinations thereof are not really relevant to every country. In such a situation, sentences such as "The first order condition is a polity that supports capital markets" or "The American polity supports capital markets" or "A polity changes and becomes receptive to markets" are exceedingly vague (for instance, "polities" do not think or act as one), almost to the point of begging the question, because any factor other than legal origins could be implicated in the efficiency of financial systems.[16] Roe's references to actual cases provide some clarification: "Property owners long dominated the state in Britain," or "Some nations, as a matter of policy and politics, support labor markets and ignore stock markets, presumably because labor interests dominate or influence their governments whereas finance-oriented property interests do not."[17] Roe and Siegel's discussion of Raghuram Rajan and Luigi Zingales's argument that market incumbents resist the entry of newcomers if it threatens the status quo and hence their interests similarly identifies a specific causal mechanism linking politics to market outcomes.[18]

The statements quoted above nonetheless raise yet another series of questions. How did it transpire that labor came to dominate—relative to financial capital—in certain countries and not others? What allows incumbents to "resist the entry of newcomers"? To be more specific, what are the institutional features of any society or polity that allow certain groups more power than others? Clearly, the answers to all these questions bear on the efficiency of financial markets. The questions are difficult to answer without systematically articulating a distinct alternative theoretical framework (as opposed to preparing a list of factors), a task that the critics of the legal origins argument do not take on. Thus, even if economic incentives are cited as factors, a more complete explanation demands the specification of the ways in which actors' interests translate to political and economic outcomes. What is needed is a historically sensitive theoretical argument that can somehow make sense of empirical descriptions that apparently go against the expectations of the legal origins framework.

This book has proposed, among other things, that the efficiency of financial markets is incidental to some of the factors discussed above, chief among which is the expected distributional implications of laws and institutions for (presumably powerful) actors or groups. If Knight is correct that "the main goal of those who develop institutional rules is to gain strategic advantage vis-à-vis other actors," then institutional rules, once established, should tend to favor certain actors or groups relative to—or even at the expense of—others.[19] Beginning with this insight, this book constructed a theoretical argument that showed how institutional rules directly translate into power asymmetries. It also demonstrated how these asymmetries themselves were contingent on the relative bargaining power of groups *before* the formation of institutions. This dynamic gives those advantaged by institutional rules both the ability and the incentive to maintain the status quo to the extent that it is advantageous to them. To put it in theoretical language, while institutions were initially endogenous to power relationships, they could also subsequently become sources of power asymmetries themselves.[20] But in order to apprehend the genesis of asymmetries due to institutional position, it is necessary to understand institutional origins.

A framework such as the one proposed in this book—also often referred to as "path dependent" in political science and sociology, emphasizing the importance of historical sequences—has certain theoretical and methodological implications. Methodologically, cross-country regressions are not ideal for testing such arguments because they cannot easily control for power relationships, which are often sequentially embedded in preexisting institutions.[21] A better alternative is a careful analysis of historical sequences over time. A second implication is that if the objective is to comprehend the relative effects of legal codes, it is problematic to pool countries without regard to their institutional histories. This follows directly from two closely related points of criticism of the legal origins argument: (1) power relationships are likely to overwhelm whatever effects legal codes per se might have, and (2) empirically, legal origins arguments do not methodologically control for the effects of such relationships.

The work of Roe and Siegel hints at and, importantly, empirically demonstrates the problems arising out of indiscriminately grouping together countries with heterogeneous institutional histories. However, these scholars do not systematically articulate an alternative or point out the theoretical (as opposed to empirical) reasons why such groupings may be a problem. For instance, they demonstrate that the relationship between legal origins and financial market development does not hold for countries that are still undeveloped (i.e., the non–Organization for Economic Co-operation and Development, or OECD, world).[22] Roe observes that this is to be expected, because developing countries have considerably "weaker basic institutions" such as "contract and property rights."[23] In effect, what he seems to be saying is that given certain "basic institutions," legal origins might marginally matter for financial development.[24] The comparability of countries for the purposes of evaluating the legal origins framework, in other words, rests on whether they have these fundamental institutions.[25]

Yet there is something seemingly arbitrary in citing "basic institutions" as *the* attribute that should determine comparability. For one thing, it is not clear what these institutions are beyond "contract and property rights." Even property rights are a problematic basis for the relevant distinction, especially given the importance of historical perspectives in explaining financial development. One cannot take the *now existing* state of property rights as a criterion to adjudicate comparability, when these rights may be the outcome of long-term historical developments. Currently developed countries have also historically massively violated property rights.[26] Further, since these basic institutions also seem to have major effects on financial development, it is imperative to identify and explain their provenance.

The power-based framework I propose here has the advantage of clearly articulating a theoretical reason for the comparability of cases, while at the same time accounting for the causes of poorly developed financial systems. According to this framework, the relevant difference between contrasting cases concerns the variation in power relationships between rulers and capital holders: institutions are manifestations of these relationships, and these differences in relationships might lead to the differences in situations that render some countries now developed and others still developing. Moreover, these initial relationships—precisely because they become congealed in institutions—cause countries to proceed on divergent paths so that comparisons yield fewer theoretical insights the further one proceeds in time. This is because preexisting institutions themselves become sources of power and perforce have an effect on subsequent institutional development.

Some examples, taken from the literature on legal origins and the scholarly discussion related to it, should illustrate the points made in the previous two paragraphs. In critiquing the legal origins framework, Rajan and Zingales observe—again based on data aggregated across multiple countries—that civil-law countries were actually more financially advanced (when measured by the stock-market-to-GDP ratio) in 1913 than common-law countries.[27] They therefore contend that the relationship between legal origins and finance holds for only the twentieth century. La Porta, Lopez-de-Silanes, and Shleifer point out, in response, that Rajan and Zingales's sample contains such curiosities as Cuba and Egypt, both of which are ranked highly on financial development but had financial sectors that were almost completely foreign. In the case of Cuba, many of the companies listed had almost nothing to do with indigenous Cuban capital formation. As La Porta, Lopez-de-Silanes, and Shleifer put it for the largest company listed, "Concerns of Havana Electric shareholders would have been addressed by either New Jersey courts or the U.S. marines."[28]

La Porta, Lopez-de-Silanes, and Shleifer are implicitly arguing that grouping together countries like Cuba and Egypt, which did not have *their own* developed capital markets, with France and United States does not really make for a good sample from which to draw theoretical conclusions about legal origins. Thus, they assert, "Perhaps a better way to get at this issue is to compare the two mother countries: England and France."[29] What they seem to be arguing here is that for countries that have their own, indigenous capital markets, legal codes seem to explain further variation; this again points to the importance of explaining the emergence of (indigenous) financial systems.

Similarly, among countries where power relationships led to the development of indigenous and institutionalized financial markets, the effects of other factors, such as the ones Roe discusses, are arguably also path dependent (that is, their effects are predicated on preexisting institutional configurations) in the manner discussed above. To take Roe's example, the impact of World War II on different European countries was conditional on their preexisting institutions. After the war, "Labour did *not* seek to displace Britain's *already* well-developed financial markets," partly because "the . . . City was itself a powerful interest group that could resist change."[30] Similarly, he points out that even at the height of leftist ascendency, the financial markets remained relatively unaffected. This, Roe, recognizes, was because these institutions "*already existed.*"[31] The more fundamental point is not their existence per se but the fact that their existence grants certain actors and groups a strategic advantage vis-à-vis others (or, alternatively, is a manifestation of their relative strategic advantage), much in the manner Knight has argued.[32] Roe's statement about the City (the financial industry) being a "powerful interest group" is better read in this sense. On the other hand, another reason Roe cites for the persistence of the financial system is problematic: he states that "it was easier for Britain to maintain an already extant private capital market," but "easier for Britain" is difficult to give precise meaning to without further clarification and elaboration.[33]

A power-based framework has the potential not only to offer a theoretically sound basis for the comparability of situations by designating defensible contrast cases but also to answer questions that the legal origins framework cannot. For instance, in order to explain the variation in the implementation of French legal codes outside France, La Porta Lopez-de-Silanes, and Shleifer observe: "The developing countries into which the French legal system was transplanted apparently adhered faithfully to the Napoleonic vision. In those countries, judges stuck to the letter of the code, resolving disputes based on formalities even when the law needed refinement."[34] It is never explained why the judges in other countries should decide to stick "to the letter of the code" while in France they showed considerable flexibility. The answer popular in the legal origins literature is ascribed to John Merryman's contention that "when the French exported their system, they did not include the information that it really does not work that way, and failed to include the blueprint of how it actually does work."[35] This is not an explanation but rather an assertion that the French were flexible because they learned from experience, while the others failed to learn from theirs.

To summarize the discussion so far, the legal origins framework has two interrelated sets of problems, one theoretical and the other epistemological. Theoretically, it cannot account for why presumably rational, self-interested individuals would follow rules that contradict their interests. And even when it cites something like habit or socialization—rather than rational egoism—as an answer, it never clarifies why the same set of culture-induced rules and codes should lead to different outcomes in different settings, especially if codes are assumed to be autonomous in the sense explained earlier. Moreover, the posited causal mechanisms of the framework do not operate as proponents claim; in other words, the framework fails to *explain*.

The second, related problem is epistemological. The argument is not able to empirically demonstrate that legal origin is either independent of or nonmarginal to power relationships. This limitation is evidenced by the fact that, as Roe and Siegel demonstrate, the relationship posited by the framework does not really hold true for the developing world. Yet critics of the legal origins argument do not clearly articulate an alternative framework beyond citing, under the heading of "political economy," a series of factors that might be relevant but are often disparate.[36] The problem with this approach is that it risks reprising some of the weaknesses of the legal origins argument by averaging a set of heterogeneous, even mutually inconsistent, causal mechanisms.[37] Yet one implicit critique of the legal origins framework is precisely that it aggregates unlike cases (that is, cases that differ enough in one dimension to render all others irrelevant or marginal at best). But criteria for what can be considered like or unlike are not pretheoretical, and neither is the methodological approach to be followed: it is theory that indicates which objects should or should not be compared and, indeed, which methodology is suited to the task. Lacking a clearly articulated alternative, therefore, any such criterion must be arbitrary, which would tend to blunt the original criticism leveled at the legal origins argument. The power-based argument provides a criterion for comparability and the methodological approach most suitable for such an investigation.

Other (Colonial) Institutional Legacies

Colonial legacies also feature in arguments that causally link such legacies with various institutions, principally relating to property rights, and then with long-term economic growth.[38] The power-based framework implies that colonialism per se is not a necessary condition for the poor development of financial markets; what matters is the power relationship underlying colonialism. What is required for an explanation is a precise specification of the particular legacies: the conditions and mechanisms that lead from colonialism to the poor development of markets, including the actors involved, their relative bargaining powers, and the interactions that lead to the relevant outcome(s). This also is the reason why one must look back in time to examine the origins of institutions rather than simply taking them as given.

One influential strand of the literature emphasizing the importance of such legacies stems from the work of Acemoglu, Johnson, and Robinson.[39] They argue that colonialism had important effects on the long-term growth of per-capita income through two distinct institutional mechanisms.[40] The emergence of growth-producing institutions, they assert, can be linked to the strategies of European colonists.

These strategies, in turn, were a function of their mortality rate in the target colony as well as its existing prosperity, as measured by urbanization and population density.[41] Europeans disproportionately settled in colonies where their mortality rate due to diseases and other factors was low, bringing with them European-style institutions "with strong emphasis on private property and checks against government power," which, in turn, led to economic growth.[42] On the other hand, where mortality rates were high, Europeans set up "extractive" institutions: "authoritarian and absolutist states with the purpose of solidifying their control and facilitating the extraction of resources."[43] Both kinds of institution could be expected to persist because, as explained in Chapters 1 and 2, the groups these institutions empowered had both strong incentives and the ability to see to it that they did. Acemoglu, Johnson, and Robinson explain the same basic point slightly differently by contending that the ruling elites empowered by the colonial rule in extractive states were generally small, and "this narrow group often was the one to control the state after independence and favored extractive institutions."[44] Another reason for persistence was that since setting up limited or government-restricting institutions was costly, it might not "pay the elites at independence to switch to extractive institutions," since the costs of setting up these institutions had already been paid by the colonial power. For the same reason (the high costs of establishing limited institutions), the elites in charge of extractive institutions at the time of independence might find it easier to continue with them. Contrary to this, settler institutions protecting property rights favored other actors whose interests were tied to their investments, which depended on such rights being upheld.[45]

The second argument Acemoglu, Johnson, and Robinson make assumes the above logic of persistence, but contends that whether or not there were widespread European settlements was also a function of the population density and relative prosperity of the target colony during the period of colonization. Institutions supporting private property rights emerged in areas of relative poverty and hence lower population density, while owing to the relative profitability of these areas, extractive institutions were either established or continued in densely populated and relatively prosperous areas.[46] This argument does not preclude the role of mortality rates in institutional development; it only suggests an additional reason why certain institutions may or may not have developed.[47]

Though the arguments above do not focus on particular institutions and seek ultimately to explain divergences in per-capita income, they have obvious implications for the subject of this study. Since their argument refers to institutions of private property rights, it should also apply to capital markets. Thus, Thorsten Beck, Asli Demirgüç-Kunt, and Ross Levine find that one of the variables associated with the explanation tendered by Acemoglu, Johnson, and Robinson (European settler mortality rate) is also positively related to the development of capital markets.[48] Yet my study suggests different possible mechanisms from those advanced by Acemoglu, Johnson, and Robinson, though there are some overlaps.

The first difference is that the theoretical framework I have presented here assumes the existence of sizable groups of merchants and traders in areas that were to become colonies, and therefore applies to regions, such as the Indian subcontinent, that satisfied this criterion. In other words, the regions that met this criterion may also have been relatively prosperous by the indicators used by Acemoglu, Johnson, and Robinson, but this may not have been necessarily the case. This means that Acemoglu, Johnson, and Robinson and Beck, Demirgüç-Kunt, and Levine could be grouping heterogeneous mechanisms that could lead to the same outcome.

Thus, in the subset of cases that satisfy the criterion of having mercantile communities, the effects of colonialism might manifest in mechanisms that are different from those suggested by Acemoglu, Johnson, and Robinson, though resulting in similar institutional and, in the long run, developmental outcomes. If the mechanism they suggest was operative in India, we should have seen evidence that the propensity of Europeans to settle was determined by the two factors they allude to. We should have found evidence that high mortality rates and preexisting population density deterred Europeans from settling in large numbers. In fact, however, the evidence indicates that the two factors were irrelevant. First, as Chapter 4 argued, both the Crown and British creditors wanted to intentionally preclude European settlements and the mixing of Europeans with natives in order to prevent an outcome akin to the American Revolution.[49] This would seem to have little to do with mortality rates, relative prosperity, or population density in the colonies. More importantly, another piece of evidence counts strongly against the crucial link between the propensity of Europeans to settle and the emergence of growth-producing institutions. As Chapter 4 demonstrated, the emergence of a contemporaneously modern banking system was very much a possibility but was thwarted because the EIC was unwilling to cede any monetary authority to local financial capital holders; moreover, the Company could afford to discount the preferences of local financial capital holders because of their superior bargaining power. It would be a very tenuous claim indeed to cast this as somehow related to the propensity of Europeans to settle.

At least in the case of capital markets, property rights would seem to be the outcome of strategic interactions between potential rulers and financial capital holders rather than just a decision problem for would-be European colonists. For such formal market institutions, the crucial factors were the primary sources of finance and revenue for the state, whether colonial or not. Consider, for instance, the case of India discussed in Chapter 4. If the British government and the creditors in the London financial market had not continued to support the colonial state in India, the Company might have had to turn to native financial capital holders, especially since the returns from land and from the government monopoly on opium trade were increasingly insufficient to support the government's wars and other conflicts throughout the nineteenth century. The situation in that case would probably have been quite propitious for the kind of arrangement that Sir James Steuart envisaged between the state and native financial capital holders, which could have resulted in the formation of a formal state-connected and state-supported money market.

There was a very different outcome in the United States. It was in numerous ways a dissimilar setting, but even here no financial markets developed as long as British creditors backed by the Crown financially supported the government of the colonies. It is quite plausible that, to the extent that the American Revolution could be considered endogenous to the explanation tendered here, it was partly the result of the refusal of the Crown and creditors to bear the bulk of the net costs of governing the colony. The emergence of a state-supported money market, then, was predicated on the primary sources of financial resources being either directly or indirectly connected to mercantile activities.

Assuming that Acemoglu, Johnson, and Robinson's general argument also applies to financial institutions, one might expect areas of relative prosperity in the seventeenth and eighteenth centuries that had a substantial class of native merchants to correlate with a lack of substantial European settlements and the subsequent emergence of deleterious institutions. The reason for this association could be that pre-European states in such areas were less likely to depend on mercantile wealth than on what they could extract from land. In addition, the colonial states that emerged were also likely to be independent of native merchants, since their ventures were generally financially supported by creditors in their "home" financial centers. On the other hand, colonial states were also likely to inherit the institutional tendencies of their predecessors insofar as their greatest domestic source of resources remained tied to land. Thus, for instance, as in the case of India, colonial rulers were likely to be favorable to the property rights of landowners and others who controlled the major domestic resources, just like their predecessors. The other side of this coin would have been their indifference (though not necessarily outright hostility) to the interests of native financial capital holders, resulting in a stunted institutional formation as far as the capital markets were concerned. Areas of relative poverty during the same period were likely to initially rely on the same "home" financial centers to finance settlement institutions. Yet in the long run, such areas were also likely to develop salubrious financial institutions to the extent that the government's main resource sources were tied to mercantile activities rather than land (as was likely when trade and the like with the mother country preceded land ownership, expansion, and development) and creditors in the "home" country refused to continue to bear the net costs of colonial governance indefinitely.

The second difference is that Acemoglu, Johnson, and Robinson's arguments are stated at too high a level of abstraction to carefully account for institutional design or detect institutional variation. This, in turn, has further implications for the relationship of colonial legacies to property rights. For instance, Acemoglu, Johnson, and Robinson group together measures for risk of expropriation, constraints on the executive, and a democracy index as signifying the nature of what they call "political" institutions.[50] But the concomitant emergence of constraints on government power, including over expropriation, and political contestation (which was narrow, due to highly restricted franchise) could have been the peculiar legacy of the historical period in question. There is no theoretical reason why strong private property protections by the state cannot coexist with authoritarian (i.e., non-democratic or not based on broad contestation) institutions, especially since the latter, by restricting direct public participation in economic policy, could actually enhance credibility to investors. In any case, the task is then to clearly account for situations under which rulers constructing state institutions are likely to strongly favor private property rights, which also has positive implications for the growth of state-supported capital markets.

Also related to the level of abstraction, Acemoglu, Johnson, and Robinson seem to refer to a universal notion of property rights in all their arguments.[51] But such rights could vary by institutional setting. The state could, while strongly protecting the property rights of one group, choose not to accord the same protection to others; thus, the colonial state in India especially defended landlords' property rights while destroying those of native financiers. This can account for the apparently contradictory evidence of the massive violation of certain kinds of property rights in the history of many now developed countries.[52] More generally, it could also be useful to see such rights as situated within a continuum ranging from state or ruler predation to ruler cooperation, with indifference lying in the middle. Merchants and bankers in India did not suffer from a lack of private property rights; indeed, it is doubtful that merchants could have grown wealthy to the extent that they did without such rights in the first place. However, these rights were not necessarily due to any positive action on the part of the state: the evidence suggests that merchants had their own codes with their own punishment mechanisms that did not include state participation. In other words, the state was notable more for its indifference than anything else. On the other hand, *zamindars* were actively given strong property rights, first by the Mughal state and then by the British colonial state. When compared to the situation of merchants and bankers in the United States, the difference was therefore not about private property rights per se but about the magnitude of those rights. Local financial investors in the United States, having the active coercive backing of the state, had far more under their control than their counterparts in India. Owing to their partnership with rulers, they could have a considerable influence over the future state of their societies, especially relative to their counterparts in the Indian subcontinent. This manifested as the development of large and thriving capital markets. Finally, this story of financial systems can potentially be generalized to other areas of the economy by noting the degree of formality of property rights through an examination of how the benefits of state coercion are distributed among actors both within and between countries.

Notes

ACKNOWLEDGMENTS

1. Russell 1932, 77.

CHAPTER I

1. An example of commercial paper would be the bill of exchange, versions of which were in use in both Asia and Europe to transfer funds over long distances.

2. Discounting involved deducting a specific percentage from the face value of bills presented.

3. See Habib 1964, 1982b.

4. Sylla, Tilly, and Tortella 1999, 1.

5. Cameron 1967, 1972; Sylla 1975; Sylla, Tilly, and Tortella 1999.

6. For one example, see La Porta, Lopez-de-Silanes, and Shleifer 2008, 307–308, 310–311.

7. These discussions began with Douglass C. North and Robert Paul Thomas's (1976) early work.

8. Very briefly, rational egoism implies that agents care only about their self-interests and are efficient (that is, use the least costly means) in pursuing them.

9. North and Weingast 1989, 806–808. Loosely, discounting the future implies valuing it less than an earlier point in time. So in this context rulers (for any reason) could value expropriation now, over a stable source of revenue for a long period of time into the future. This is somewhat analogous to the fable of the goose that laid golden eggs.

10. Ibid., 821.

11. Stock of payment medium refers to (the total amount of) all instruments, including of course bank notes, that count as a means of payment in transactions.

12. The two banks in question were federally chartered banks that also held the government's deposits. President Jackson vetoed a vote confirming a renewal of the charter of the second Bank of the United States. The first Bank of the United States' charter renewal fell short by one vote in both the House and the Senate.

13. Counterfactuals, roughly, are statements that say what would have happened had things been different in specified ways. The difficulty of empirically substantiating such propositions arises from the fact that things were not different, and hence the predicted world (had things been different) did not come to pass.

CHAPTER 2

1. Haber, Razo, and Maurer 2003; Haber, North, and Weingast 2008. Indeed, as shown below, some of North's own subsequent work, including with his collaborators, seems to imply this interpretation.

2. North and Weingast 1989, 804.

3. Ibid.

4. Stasavage 2002 (155–156), 2007 (124–126).

5. Stasavage 2007.

6. An additional possibility is that partisan control interacted with the establishment of institutions such as the Bank of England (as I argue below). Indeed, Stasavage (2002, 164) would seem to imply as much.

7. North and Weingast 1989, 821, quoting Macaulay 1914, 2438.

8. For a more recent commentary on this phenomenon in the context of the rise of finance in the United States, see Greta Krippner's argument (2011, 144–150) that the depoliticization of the economy involves simultaneous ideational *and* institutional change.

9. This situation would avoid the credibility problems inherent in "open access systems" (North, Wallis, and Weingast 2009, 21–27).

10. Haber, Razo, and Maurer 2003, 36.

11. Ibid., 37–38. See note 9 in the previous chapter.

12. Ibid., 31.

13. North 1990, 58–59.

14. This presumption of set-ups based in game theory has been noted, and questioned, by Terry Moe (2005).

15. Knight 1992, 41. Knight further urges that this understanding of power asymmetries be incorporated into standard rational choice frameworks (which normally assume that agents are equally powerful). This point is repeated in Moe 2005.

16. Knight 1992, 131–136.

17. Richard Emerson (1962) also suggested this formulation of power.

18. Tilly 1992, 27.

19. This scenario assumes that capital holders are confronted with only one set of rulers. The situation would remain substantially unchanged even if merchants and bankers had access to multiple *potential* rulers within the same political unit, because the availability of resources for any potential rulers would remain unchanged. Every

aspirant or set of aspirants would have to be primarily concerned with the sources that yielded them maximum financial resources. One could offer further theoretical speculations about the conditions under which divisions among rulers would be mitigated as they reached stable revenue-sharing agreements and formed stable coalitions, but that is not directly relevant to the argument here.

20. Variable discount rate refers to the possibility that rulers could (for many reasons) stop valuing the proceeds of long-term cooperation with investors. Also see note 9 in Chapter 1.

21. See Hardin 1997, chap. 2.

22. North and Weingast 1989, 825.

23. Knight 1992, 40.

24. They could do this by credibly threatening retaliation; their threat would be credible because of the institutional status quo, as discussed earlier.

25. The argument here abstracts away from specific forms of government, but the assumption that rulers would not face equivalent collective-action problems is defensible even where there is regular or irregular rotation of leaders, as long as they have certain executive abilities (including those of advancing policy proposals) by virtue of their institutional position.

26. "Destructive" reflects the perspective of incumbents, putting aside for the moment the question of what should, from a societal perspective, be the optimum level of competition and regulation in the money market.

27. Thus, for instance, when the state in England invited its creditors to incorporate as the Bank of England and made some institutional changes, this greatly facilitated mutual cooperation *among* individual creditors, in addition to serving as an act of cooperation *between* rulers and financiers/creditors. More generally, any act of cooperation with an entity such as the state under conditions where the state's chief source of finances is linked to merchants and bankers provides added incentives for individual financial capital holders to form groups (where such groupings do not exist already), because, for one thing, it reduces the risks associated with individual cooperation.

28. For an analogue in another market that also has some interesting differences, in the sense that the problem manifests in market competition and not with respect to regulation, see Bowman 2006.

29. This is yet another variation on the general theme, first suggested by E. E. Schattschneider (1935, 288), that "new policies create new politics."

30. See, e.g., Hoffmann 2001; Lomazoff 2012, 1–23.

31. Weber 1946, 280.

32. The literature on historical institutionalism has also noted that ideas and interests need not be considered mutually exclusive. See, e.g., Steinmo 2008, 130–131.

33. Hoffmann 2001, 56.

34. Ibid., 59.

35. Consider the observations of Paul Studenski and Herman E. Kroos (1952, 2) on this matter. They argue that during this period the expectation was that the

government, "while expected not to interfere with business in any way . . . was required to furnish a variety of aids to business . . . [and thus to] be a subsidiary agent which should respond to business commands and give business every support required." See also Hartz 1948.

36. See Chapter 5; for Duane's version of the events, see Duane 1838.

37. *Report No. 283*, 22nd Cong., 1st sess., 1832, 30–31; the report quoted here, an earlier one presented on April 13, 1830, was appended to the 1832 report, which was also supportive of the Bank of the United States.

38. Hoffmann 2001, 65.

39. *H.R. Doc. No. 2*, 23rd Cong., 1st sess., 1833, 34.

40. Hoffmann 2001, 65–69. Jackson's "specie circular" was an executive order stipulating that the government would accept only gold and silver, and not banknotes, as payment for land purchases.

41. Studenski and Kroos 1952, 120. For the relationship between the government and merchants and bankers, see Cohen 1971. For a summary of all the problems, see Kinley 1893, esp. chap. 3.

42. On the importance of the institutional environment in shaping the preferences of political actors regarding outcomes, see Thelen and Steinmo 1992, 1–32.

43. As Hoffmann herself notes (2001, 12), the "liberal" philosophy of Jefferson and Jackson was later claimed both by such theorists as Milton Friedman and Robert Nozick (along with other defenders of the corporate form) and by the nineteenth-century populists. At the same time, this different reception and transmogrification of the same basic philosophy (and the subsequent prominence of neoliberalism, rather than populist liberalism) cannot be explained without reference to power configurations.

44. Krippner 2011, 144–150.

45. Ibid., 145.

46. This is suggested in Krippner's broader argument that the deregulation of the financial market was the result of a series of responses that policy makers made to certain crises beginning in the 1970s. The role of powerful social groups is implicit in much of her discussion. For instance, she notes that one of the reasons for the fiscal crisis was that "although private industry was the ultimate beneficiary of state spending, capitalists were not willing to pay for these expenditures through increased taxation" (2011, 18).

47. Knight 1992, 45.

48. Ibid., 28.

49. Hammond 1957; Mihm 2007, 125–134. Hoffmann (2001, 43) also attributes the failure to recharter the first Bank to a coalition of those opposing it on principle and those desiring cheap money.

50. Counterfactuals—or contrary-to-fact conditionals—cannot be literally true or false, just more or less plausible. The philosophical literature linking counterfactuals and causation is quite extensive. For an introduction, see Lewis 1993, 193–204.

51. T. Ferguson 1995, 28.

52. This criticism is somewhat less applicable to the period of extensive public polling, since evidence for realistic or counterfactually possible alternative positions can be demonstrated by showing the general popularity of certain policy positions in opinion polls. Nevertheless, whether investors perceived such positions as going against their vital interests, notwithstanding the general popularity of these positions, would remain to be shown

53. Stated slightly differently, the evidence presented shows mainly that major party positions inevitably received the support of a major faction of investors. See T. Ferguson 1995.

54. Again, see Schattschneider 1935, 288.

55. Of course, this is not a particularly original observation: much writing and research in economic sociology is based on this premise. See, e.g., Smelser and Swedberg 1994; Fligstein 2002; Polanyi 1957. One might further conceive of interests and institutions as mutually constitutive; in fact, Krippner's (2011) argument could be interpreted in this way.

56. T. Ferguson 1995, 57.

57. Indeed, since it cannot rule out alternative conditions, this evidence would not even imply that the opposition of these bankers was *sufficient*. But this is just a methodological point arising from the difficulty of substantiating a sufficient condition from just one instance, not a problem with the theory per se. Indeed, the methodological difficulties can be ameliorated to some extent—even within the context of a single case—by demonstrating that alternative sufficient conditions were not present at the right time or place, thus ruling them out.

58. Hoffmann (2001, 58) also notes this, but interprets it as demonstrating the importance of Jackson's public philosophy. But, as argued at length in the previous section, this constitutes a partial explanation at best.

59. Levy 2008, 629; see also note 50 above.

60. There can be various kinds of counterfactuals, and the empirical appraisal of such statements depends on their nature. It should suffice here to point out that appraisal is crucially dependent on the precision with which the antecedent conditions and alternative world are described. Indeed, counterfactuals are generally sensitive to contrast cases. For a longer discussion, see A. Chatterjee 2013, 85–87; Levy 2008.

61. Again, the political science literature on these methodological issues is now quite extensive. For an overview, see ibid. and Box-Steffensmeier, Brady, and Collier 2008.

62. The second part, concerning developments within an already institutionalized system, is relevant to the extension of the original theoretical framework as discussed in the section titled "Additional Implications, or an Extension of the Argument."

63. Of course, the very notions of similarity and difference rest on theoretical considerations. They depend on which factors one considers theoretically relevant

in explaining phenomena, and empirical demonstrations aim at substantiating the causal relevance of these factors. Demonstrating that the theory has correctly identified the relevant causal factors is just another way of making the same epistemological point: that is, it shows that despite differences in many other dimensions, the factors identified in the theory succeed in explaining the relevant outcomes.

64. I say "plausible" because, again, counterfactuals cannot be literally true or false; see also note 50 above.

65. For an example of a similar method of argumentation, see Carpenter 2008.

CHAPTER 3

1. Sylla 2000, 497.

2. Hammond 1957, 144–145.

3. Brock 1975, 5–7.

4. Ibid. See also Ernst 1973, chap. 2; E. J. Ferguson 1961, 4.

5. Ernst 1973, 21. See also Brock 1975, 17–18.

6. Brock 1975, 18.

7. Studenski and Kroos 1952, 17.

8. These institutions issued currency on loans backed by land mortgages. See Ernst 1973, xvii. See also Thayer 1953.

9. Brock 1975, 17–20; Ernst 1973, 24–30.

10. This is because the credit extended also allowed colonists to buy British goods. Brock (1975, 185) also notes this.

11. Ibid., 19.

12. It is interesting here to see how a dynamic that Stasavage (2002, 2007) identifies in the context of an already existing institutionalized (that is, state-connected) money and credit system operates in a very different context: the absence of those institutions. As discussed later in this chapter, evidence from the northern colonies shows that the legislative assemblies, whose memberships were mostly quite restricted, that were reliably controlled by financial capital holders generally retained the power to issue a payment medium, while the relatively more democratic legislative assemblies enacted versions of the private constraint—by, for instance, establishing gold as the only medium of payment—as soon as holders of financial capital (temporarily) controlled them.

13. See Brock 1975, 232–239; E. J. Ferguson 1961, 11; Ernst 1973, 39.

14. See Brock 1975, 220–228.

15. See Greene and Jellison 1961, 485–518; Ernst 1973, esp. 89–133, 207–215. For differences between the 1751 and 1764 acts, see Ernst 1973, 86.

16. Brock 1975, 224–225, 228–230; the quote (see 224) refers to Pennsylvania. Making a similar observation about New York, Brock points out: "New York's strategy was similar to that of Pennsylvania" (1975, 225).

17. Ernst 1973, 308–311.

18. For a very general introduction to the various colonial assemblies, see Greene 1961, 451–474.

19. The concern here is not with democracy per se, which is a far broader issue involving both empirical and conceptual questions, but with merchant representation. In the absence of direct evidence, tracing geographical residence and representation seems to be the best method of making such inferences. See R. E. Brown 1952, 291–313, esp. 305–307.

20. R. E. Brown 1953, 464.

21. Ibid., 467, 472.

22. See Zemsky 1969, 508.

23. Zemsky calls those who collectively held half the committee assignments "major leaders" and those who held the next 25 percent of all the assignments "subleaders" (ibid., 503).

24. R. E. Brown 1952, 305. Zemsky (1969, 508) assumes that all representatives from the seaports spoke for the "merchant community."

25. R. E. Brown 1952, 304–306.

26. Zemsky 1969, 513.

27. Ibid., 513; R. E. Brown 1952, 304–306. Even when the Board of Trade sometimes declared certain land-bank schemes illegal, the assembly managed to get its way by passing other kinds of emissions such as bills of credit (Zemsky 1969, 519).

28. For figures on price inflation, see B. D. Smith 1985, 543. Whether the relationship between depreciation and inflation was causal during this time is a matter of some scholarly debate, but defenders of hard money would doubtless have used the correlation in their favor and might have been able to convince others of this view. For more information on the passage of the bill, see Brock 1975, 247–253; E. J. Ferguson 1961, 11.

29. For an explanation of why New England currency should be considered as one unit before 1751, see Brock 1975, 35. On efforts to prevent the bills of neighboring provinces from circulating, see also ibid., 253–256.

30. Harrington 1964, 37–46.

31. Ibid., 39–41; Levermore 1896, 239–240.

32. Levermore 1896, 239–240. Indeed, William Livingston's grandfather Robert Livingston was one of the earliest merchants of the province of New York; see Leder and Carosso 1956. For more details, see Becker 1901 (260–275), 1909.

33. Levermore 1896, 245.

34. Ibid., 245–246.

35. Lester 1939, 182. To agree with this factual statement, one need not accept Lester's argument about the effects of currency emissions on the general economic condition, especially prices and terms of trade.

36. Brock 1975, 74.

37. Leonard 1954, 388; see also ibid., 387.

38. Ibid., 387.

39. For a general profile of the members of this party, see Warden 1964, 367–389.

40. Zimmerman 1960, 292–313.

41. Newcomb 1966, 261. The Quaker Party had opposed only the means of protest. For a general view of the politics of Pennsylvania and, particularly, how the Quaker Party maintained its dominance for most of the period leading up to the revolution, see also W. R. Smith 1909, 208–213.

42. Lester 1938, 335. But even here there is evidence that plenty of wealthy merchants supported currency issuances (see ibid., 330–337, esp. the governor's letter on 336).

43. Lester 1938, 375; for the view of British merchants, see also ibid., 369.

44. Knight 1992, 41.

45. See Schlesinger 1957, 17–21.

46. The reasons for British intransigence on these issues are irrelevant to the immediate argument, but they may have had to do with diversion of British credit to other, newly acquired territories in India and the West Indies. See, e.g., Sheridan 1960.

47. A discussion of how this new (potential) governing elite emerged from the convergence of the interests of northern and middle-state merchants and southern planters as a result of the various parliamentary acts would take us too far afield from the central task of this chapter. For details of the roots of planter opposition (especially in Virginia), see Egnal 1988; Alvord 1916; Harrell 1925; Evans 1962; Tate 1962; Curtis 1972. Arthur Schlesinger (1957) notes the coincidence of interests among both planters and merchants against these parliamentary acts.

48. For details, see Schlesinger 1957; Tyler 1986; Oaks 1977; Egnal and Ernst 1972, 4–32; Ryerson 1974, 561–588; Egnal 1988; Countryman 1981.

49. Wicker 1985, 877.

50. Ibid., 877, 874.

51. E. J. Ferguson 1961, 26.

52. Quoted in Bezanson 1951, 27.

53. Ibid.

54. E. J. Ferguson 1961, 30.

55. For an idea of the difficulties involved in ascertaining the probability of French support, see Corwin 1915, 33–61.

56. McCusker 1972, 152.

57. Schlesinger 1957, 595–598.

58. Quoted in Main 1963, 38.

59. Quoted in Schlesinger 1957, 599.

60. Quoted in ibid.

61. For some examples see Doerflinger 1983 (197–226), 1986 (esp. chap. 4); Schlesinger 1957, 594; Oaks 1970.

62. Main 1963, 33.

63. Of course, all this does not preclude mistakes on the part of the merchants choosing one side or the other. For example, individual merchants could predict the progress of the revolution wrongly and consequently declare allegiance to the weaker side.

64. Egnal 1988, 310.

65. Tyler 1986, 241–251, 258–277; Young 1987, 126; Harrington 1964, 349–350; Countryman 1981, 114; Oaks 1970, 206.

66. Tiedmann 1984, 1986, 1988.

67. Tiedmann 1984, 60.

68. Ibid., 67.

69. Moreover, many of the merchants would have been familiar with the Bank of England, which would have acted as a model of the kind of institution that could solve, or at least allay, some of their concerns.

70. See E. J. Ferguson 1961, chap. 3; Mason 1966, 190–212.

71. E. J. Ferguson 1961, 51, 57–69.

72. Quoted in ibid., 112; see also Hammond 1957, 44.

73. East 1969, 206–209; Harlow 1929, 63–65; Handlin and Handlin 1947, 23–26.

74. East 1969, 208.

75. Compare the list of Whig merchants in Oaks 1970 (216–236) with the names of the ninety-seven merchants in Konkle 1937 (94–95).

76. *Journals of the Continental Congress* 17:550.

77. Hammond 1957, 43.

78. East 1969, 207–208.

79. E. J. Ferguson 1961, 123.

80. See Hammond 1957, 65–66; Redlich 1968, 25.

81. For details, see Perkins 1994, esp. 131–176; Hammond 1957, 53–64.

82. E. J. Ferguson 1961, 249.

83. McGuire 2003, 72, 86–89. The debate surrounding an "economic" interpretation of the Constitution, of course, goes back to Charles Beard's ([1913] 1935) work.

84. McGuire 2003, 88. His data is based on the probable vote from records of the convention.

85. For voting outcomes, see McGuire 2003, 255. To compare the two votes, see ibid., 88–89, where—by estimating the probability that those absent would have voted for or against the measure—McGuire imputes votes to those not actually present and voting.

86. Main 1961, 166.

87. For details, see *American State Papers, Finance*, vol. 1 (1789–1802), no. 6, "Public Credit," House of Representatives, 1st Cong., 2nd sess., 1790; ibid., no. 17, "Public Credit," House of Representatives, 1st Cong., 3rd sess., 1790.

88. Ibid., no. 18, "National Bank," House of Representatives, 1st Cong., 3rd sess., 1790.

89. Ibid., no. 19, "Public Creditors," Senate, 1st Cong., 3rd sess., 1790, 76.

90. Hammond 1957, 115.

91. Redlich 1968, 34; see also ibid., 42; Hammond 1957, 125.

92. Redlich 1968, 34.

CHAPTER 4

1. Those interested in the chronology of events should note that the death of Emperor Aurangzeb in 1707 led to a series of wars of succession, as high aristocrats in the court fought for control of the empire. This also created a situation where local rulers of provinces—formerly officers of the emperor—became more autonomous. Bengal was one such major province, with substantial European presence, including that of the East India Company. The EIC's presence there dated to the early years of the eighteenth century. The Company secured *zamindari*—that is, became a landlord—of substantial portions of Bengal after its victory in the Battle of Plassey in 1757. It further became the revenue collector and de facto ruler of most of the present-day states of Bengal (including the country of Bangladesh), Bihar, and Orissa (these were consolidated as the Presidency of Bengal under the EIC) after its victory in the Battle of Buxar in 1764. The next text section (titled "The Counterfactual") refers to subsequent events.

2. This designation succeeded the position of "governor," of which there were four in succession prior to the creation of the governor general's office.

3. For Bengal's lucrative reputation, and the basis for this, see Bernier 1891, 202, 437–442; S. Chaudhuri 1975, 1. For the EIC's expectations, see Bowen 2005, 4–5.

4. Marshall 1976, 158, among others. He uses the term "loot."

5. Mitra 1991, 24; see also Marshall 1976, 179.

6. Harry Verelst, the second governor general, estimated that Bengal lost over £8,000,000 in bullion. See Verelst 1772, 79–81, 86.

7. J. C. Sinha 1925, 47; Mitra 1991, 28–29.

8. For Verelst's view, see 1772, 94–95.

9. J. C. Sinha 1925, 48.

10. Verelst 1772, 94–95.

11. Mitra 1991, 70–90.

12. Ibid., 39–40.

13. K. Chatterjee 1996, 197; Mitra 1991, 40.

14. Mitra 1991, 40; K. Chatterjee 1996, 198.

15. K. Chatterjee 1996, 198–199.

16. Mitra 1991, 58.

17. K. Chatterjee 1996, 200, 220.

18. Furber 1948, 242–243. It is difficult to determine the exact amount, though some estimates exist. The latest one is by Javier Esteban (2001), who estimates that the Company imported bullion worth about £326,000 between 1793 and 1802 and about £645,000 between 1803 and 1807. Compare these figures to his estimates of £98,000 between 1784 and 1792 and a mere £26,000 for the entire period between 1772 and 1783.

19. K. Chatterjee 1996, 201–202; Bagchi 1985, 503.

20. Keynes 1913, 195–196.

21. Mitra 1991, 44.

22. This process of demonetization was subsequently repeated in other provinces as the EIC gained control over them. See Bayly 1983, 274.

23. The only remark by historians about its nonacceptance is an offhand comment—repeated in at least two sources—that it was considered too advanced for its time, a statement that obviously does not quite constitute an argument. See J. C. Sinha 1925, 49; Mitra 1991.

24. Mitra 1991, 54.

25. Steuart 1772.

26. Ibid., 74.

27. Ibid.

28. Ibid., 77–78.

29. Ibid., 78.

30. Ibid., 79, italics added.

31. Ibid., 79–80, italics added.

32. Bayly 2000, 379.

33. Habib 1969, 73–74.

34. S. Chaudhuri 1975, 97.

35. Habib 1982b, 363, italics added.

36. Pearson 1976, 131.

37. Ibid., 119–120; Das Gupta 1982, 407–433.

38. Subramanian and Ray 1991, 19–20. For an example of this manner of payment—and an indication of how commonplace it was—see the accounts of the French merchant Jean-Baptiste Tavernier, who received such payment from Mughal nobles (Tavernier [1676] 1889, 32–34).

39. For the nature of the Mughal monetary system, see Martin 1987, esp. 93–96; Deyell 1987, 43–45; Richards 1987, 2–3.

40. For instances under Aurangzeb, see Manucci 1907, 61–62; Mallick 1991, 46–48.

41. Habib 1964, 58; Richards 1981, 292–294; Raychaudhuri 1982, 186.

42. Habib 1982a, 244–245.

43. Habib 1969 (45), 1982a (245).

44. Subrahmanyam 2001, 6.

45. Das Gupta 1982, 422.

46. For the need for short-term credit, see S. Chaudhuri 1975 (62–74), 1978 (67–68), 1988 (97–100).

47. Pearson 1976, 119–120.

48. There is some evidence, on the other hand, that during the period between the complete decline of centralized Mughal rule and the consolidation of the EIC state, localized institutional arrangements emerged between rulers and financial capital holders that were reminiscent of the credible commitments discussed earlier. These agreements emerged precisely in localities where land revenues no longer met rulers' needs. However, the arrangements did not survive the consolidation of EIC rule. See Singh 1974, 21–22; Cohn 1960, 22; Bayly 1983, 167.

49. Bhattacharya 1969, 3; Subramanian and Ray 1991.

50. Subramanian and Ray 1991, 38–39.

51. N. K. Sinha 1962, 23.

52. Ibid.

53. See, for example, Ray 2003, 235.

54. Chaudhury 1988, 98–99.

55. Dickson 1967, 407.

56. Furber 1948, 269; see also Furber 1948, 18; Dickson 1967, 234.

57. S. Chaudhuri 1975 (65, 74–82), 1988 (97–100).

58. Quoted in Chaudhury 1988, 91. See also ibid., 92; Bhattacharya 1969, 101.

59. N. K. Sinha 1961, 6–7.

60. K. N. Chaudhuri 1978, 461.

61. K. N. Chaudhuri 1985, 120.

62. Hill (1905) 1968, 1:196, 2:15, 3:161; Ray 2003, 235.

63. Hill (1905) 1968, 1:3, 1:58, 2:145.

64. Ibid., 3:175.

65. Ray 2003, 246. For a view of the events from the perspective of a local historian, see Khan 1789, 1:720–744.

66. Hill (1905) 1968, 2:383–385. R. K. Ray (2003, 246) refers to the battle as a "mock" one because the *nawab*'s bribed generals merely pretended to fight.

67. Vansittart (1766) 1976, 2:430, 2:365, 2:378–379, 2:368–370; Ray 2003, 248, 278–301.

68. Marshall 1976, 40, 43–44, 158.

69. I. B. Watson 1980, 262; Marshall 1976, 44–45.

70. For the EIC's use of banking networks, see Subramanian 1996, 146–159; for its end, see Subramanian and Ray 1991, 56; Tripathi 1979, 10–11; K. Chatterjee 1996, 192–193; Bagchi 1987, 42.

71. For the importance of land revenue, see Grant 1791, 47–51, 69–74; see also *Fifth Report from the Committee of Secrecy* 1773.

72. Bowen 2005, 4, 59. See also ibid., 17, 31; Furber 1948, 29.

73. Ingram 1970, 130–132, 190–191, 217–218.

74. Tripathi 1979, 10.

75. Ingram 1970, 191; Tripathi 1979, 62, 170.

76. The Company eventually lost its monopoly on trade with India in 1813 in return for yet another twenty-year renewal of its charter and more financial assistance. In brief, the nineteenth century saw the emergence of other trading and, shortly thereafter, manufacturing interests in Britain that were keen on preventing India from becoming a center for the production of manufactured goods; once Britain's manufacturing superiority was ensured, they intended to gain access to the Indian market. Those providing financial assistance in India were private traders and agency houses that wanted to break into the Company's monopolies. Unable to completely liquidate its debts in India, the Company instead traded increasing parts of its monopoly for financial assistance. For details, see Tripathi 1979.

77. Ibid., 151.

78. Bagchi 1987, 48.

79. Chandavarkar 1983, 774.

80. Andrew 1901, 484.

81. Goldsmith 1983, 29.

82. Hurd 1983, 749–750.

83. Ray 1992, 12; Bayly 1973, 349.

84. Ray 1992, 11; Sen 1992, 125.

85. See "Letter LV (Dundas to Wellesley)," Ingram 1970, 191.

86. Tripathi 1979, 62.

87. See Fazl (1590?) 1891, 129–412.

88. Ibid., 252.

89. Pearson 1976, 24.

90. Ibid., 24, 23.

91. Ibid., 24.

92. Elliot 1877, 138.

93. Ibid., 164.

94. N. K. Sinha 1962, 1, 3.

95. These amounts are rounded. Furber 1933, 30.

96. Furber 1948, 236.

97. Bowen 2005, 226.

98. Tripathi 1979, 100, 281.

99. Bowen 2005, 35; Furber 1948, 265, 81.

100. Furber 1948, 97. In 1806, the Company raised its bond debt by £2,000,000 while the government contributed £1,000,000, and by 1809 the government had contributed an additional £1,500,000. See ibid., 97–98.

101. Ibid., 111–113.

102. Marshall 1987, 105.

103. Calculated from Bowen 2005, 280.

Chapter 5

1. Hoffmann 2001; Hammond 1957.

2. Hammond 1957; Schlesinger Jr. (1945) 1971; Mihm 2007, 125–134.

3. T. Ferguson 1995, 28.

4. For a recent example of the use of such counterfactuals, see Carpenter 2008, 825–846. Thus, in explaining the lack of reform in the financial sector despite the popularity of such steps, he argues that "the paths not taken in this saga remain as informative as those that were followed." In effect, therefore, Carpenter's argument demonstrates the real counterfactual possibilities in the form of alternative policies that were suggested but failed for the reasons he posits. See ibid., 837.

5. This possibility is implicitly noted in a recent volume on institutional change. The authors write, "Actors disadvantaged by one institution may be able to use their advantaged status vis-à-vis other institutions to enact change." The difference between this statement and my argument is that I specify the directions in which change will *not* proceed. See Mahoney and Thelen 2010, 9.

6. The evidence comprises mainly published personal papers, newspaper articles, government documents, and petitions to Congress.

7. In this respect, my explanation differs from the one that Ferguson offers, which is based on his investment theory. For details, see the discussion in Chapter 2.

8. See the section in Chapter 2 titled "Relating This Extension to Other Arguments: Ideas, Institutions, and Power."

9. As discussed in Chapter 2, this is a version of Max Weber's formulation, which sees "elective affinities" between ideas, and interests of all kinds (that is, self-regarding, selfless/economic, and noneconomic).

10. Hammond 1957, 144–145.

11. *American State Papers, Finance*, vol. 2 (1802–1815), no. 256, "Public Deposites [*sic*] in Banks," House of Representatives, 9th Cong., 2nd sess., 1806.

12. Redlich 1968, 34.

13. Ibid., 245.

14. Ibid.

15. Wettereau 1942, 71–72.

16. Bruchey 1970, 350.

17. For examples, see Redlich 1968, 245–247; Bruchey 1970, 354–377; Holdsworth and Dewey 1910, 40–41. The same was true in Philadelphia, where, as noted previously, the Bank of North America and the Bank of Pennsylvania seem to have coexisted without any major conflicts. See Schwartz 1947, 425.

18. Quoted in Bruchey 1970, 353–354.

19. For an example drawn from the early years of the Bank, see Cowen 2000a, 1041–1060. On the other hand, some evidence exists that under the leadership of the secretary of the treasury and the Bank of the United States, the early banks worked in concert to severely curtail credit on at least one occasion. See ibid., 1052–1056. For evidence of early cooperation between the Bank and other banks and Hamilton's efforts to this end, see Cowen 2000b, chap. 3.

20. See, e.g., *American Citizen*, January 10, 1804.

21. Lamoreaux 1996, esp. 1–52. Note, however, that the argument about credit discrimination does not *necessarily* depend on evidence of insider lending. Rather, evidence of insider lending is *sufficient* for demonstrating credit discrimination.

22. See, e.g., Lamoreaux 1996, 4–5, 7–9, 25–27.

23. Redlich 1968, 22.

24. Ibid., 31–32.

25. Hammond (1957, 148) argues that this increasingly became the case during the time noted.

26. Wright 1999, 54.

27. The newspaper was the *National Intelligencer and Washington Advertiser*, published by Samuel Harrison Smith, a supporter of Jefferson in particular and the Democratic Republican Party in general. See Blodget 1804, 1.

28. Ibid.

29. *American State Papers, Finance*, vol. 2 (1802–1815), no. 283, "Bank of the United States," Senate, 10th Cong., 1st sess., 1808, 301.

30. Ibid., no. 298, "Bank of the United States," Senate, 10th Cong., 2nd sess., 1809, 351.

31. Hammond 1957, 210.

32. I could find only 3 articles (out of about 136) that came out against the banking system in general (i.e., against all privately owned banks).

33. See, e.g., "More Lies and General Smith" 1810, 2; Carey 1810, 2. The latter was printed in the *Commercial Advertiser*, which was published in New York.

34. See "United States Bank" 1810, 2; the same article was reprinted in the *Northern Whig* (see "Extract of a Letter" 1810).

35. The Philadelphia newspaper *Aurora*, run by Duane, was at the forefront of such criticisms. See Corrector 1810b, 2. The same article, also written under the pseudonym "Corrector," was reprinted in the *Old Colony Gazette* (see Corrector 1810a, 1). See also the series of articles by "Common Sense" in the Burlington newspaper *Northern Centinel* (e.g., Common Sense 1811, 1–2). The first of the three articles was republished in the Richmond-based newspaper *The Enquirer* in 1811.

36. See Commercial Capitalist of New York 1810, 1–2.

37. See, e.g., "Bank of the United States" 1811a, 2.

38. See Common Sense 1811, 1–2. Another frequent criticism of the Bank was the concern that slightly less than three-fourths of the total bank stock had passed into the hands of those living in Britain. See "The U.S. Bank, Again" 1810, 1–2; Duane's February 12, 1811, *Weekly Aurora* went so far as to call it the "British Branch bank."

39. This had been reported and criticized in Federalist newspapers. See "Crowninshield on Banks" 1806, 2–3, reprinted in the *Boston Gazette* (see "Crowninshield on Banks" 1807, 2).

40. See "The Bank of the United States" 1811b, 1.

41. *American State Papers, Finance*, vol. 2 (1802–1815), no. 344, "Bank of the United States," Senate, 11th Cong., 3rd sess., 1811, 481.

42. Ibid., no. 328, "Bank of the United States," Senate, 11th Cong., 3rd sess., 1810, 452; ibid., no. 329, "Bank of the United States," Senate, 11th Cong., 3rd sess., 1810, 453–454. See also a petition against the Bank from "Inhabitants of Pittsburgh," in ibid., no. 343, "Bank of the United States," Senate, 11th Cong., 3rd sess., 1811, 479–480.

43. Ibid., no. 333, "Bank of the United States," Senate, 11th Cong., 3rd sess., 1811, 460.

44. See Holdsworth and Dewey 1910, 83–84.

45. Ibid., 86; see also Hammond 1957, 213.

46. Holdsworth and Dewey 1910, 92. Smith repeatedly alleged that the Bank granted credit mostly to Federalists, a claim that was criticized by Federalist newspapers. See "More Lies and General Smith" 1810, 2.

47. The votes are from Clark and Hall 1832, 274, 446.

48. *The Bee* 1, no. 31 (March 8, 1811): 2.

49. See, e.g., "U.S. Bank" 1811, 2.

50. "Bank of the United States" 1810a, 2.

51. For other examples of this position, see "Union" 1811, 2.

52. *American State Papers, Finance*, vol. 2 (1802–1815), no. 298, "Bank of the United States," Senate, 10th Cong., 2nd sess., 1809, 352–353.

53. "Extract of a Letter" 1810, 2.

54. "Bank of the United States" 1810b, 2.

55. *Weekly Aurora*, October 30, 1810, 4.

56. See *Papers of James. A. Bayard* 1913, 181.

57. Quoted in Hammond 1957, 217; see also ibid., 216–219.

58. *American State Papers, Finance*, vol. 2 (1802–1815), no. 362, "Public Deposites [*sic*] in Banks," House of Representatives, 12th Cong., 1st sess., 1812, 516.

59. For a detailed description, see Walters 1945, 115–131; see also K. L. Brown 1942, 125–148.

60. Thus, for instance, one provision that was struck down allowed the U.S. president to appoint the bank's president. Another provision that was left out allowed the government to pay for its subscription with treasury notes. Yet another provision that was struck down would have prohibited the bank from selling government securities on the open market; this provision was clearly aimed at precluding the possibility that government securities would remain with only a certain group of investors. One charter that did not pass prohibited the holders of government securities from exchanging them for bank stock. Finally, one that Madison vetoed met the requirements of all financiers but failed to give the government any role. See Walters 1945, esp. 120–128; for the debates, amendments, and votes on the final bill, see Clark and Hall 1832, 619–621, 630–712. For earlier debates on various bank plans, see ibid., 481–482, 578–585.

61. Walters 1945, 124.

62. *American State Papers, Finance*, vol. 2 (1802–1815), no. 429, "Bank of the United States," House of Representatives, 13th Cong., 3rd sess., 1814, 872.

63. Clark and Hall 1832, 614, emphasis added.

64. Hoffmann 2001, 58.

65. I found one article that spoke of the need to abolish all state banks and replace them with branches of the Bank of the United States. The article also proposed that all states have representation in the new bank. See *Norwich Courier*, August 31, 1825, 3.

66. I counted over seven hundred petitions on the subject of the Bank of the United States submitted to Congress from all parts of the country between about 1832 and 1834 (between the Twenty-Second Congress, first session, and the Twenty-Third Congress, second session). The petitions prior to the autumn of 1833 primarily concerned the question of whether the Bank should be rechartered. After the executive removed government deposits from the Bank in late 1833, the petitions also addressed the propriety of this particular action. J. A. Wilburn (1967, 53) counts about 118 pro-bank memorials and petitions leading up to the president's

veto of the Bank bill in 1832. At this point there were fewer than twenty anti-Bank petitions.

67. I counted twenty-two petitions specifically from workers between 1832 and 1834. Virtually all of them were, expectedly, from the urban regions of the United States: mostly New York City, Philadelphia and its surrounding areas, and a couple of New England towns. Of these, nineteen petitions were in favor of the Bank of the United States and three were against it.

68. I counted seventy-seven petitions from banks, chartered corporations, or merchants and traders presented from shortly prior to the veto to 1834. Of these, only four opposed the Bank, including one from the New England merchant David Henshaw—whom Hammond (1957, 330, 338) cites as one of the Bank's opponents—and his associates, requesting the opportunity to incorporate another bank to replace it. Henshaw's appeal consists of assuring Congress that a repeal of the Bank's charter would cause little disruption and offering to assist in the transition. See *H.R. Doc. No. 37*, 22nd Cong., 1st sess., 1832. Of note is the absence of a petition from any state bank against the Bank and the presence of close to fifty petitions in favor, which demonstrates that Bank president Nicholas Biddle and the Bank's other allies were at least successful in keeping bankers from explicitly expressing their disapproval. For an overview of Biddle's efforts, see McGrane 1919, 122, 123–124, 125–127. Wilburn's investigation into what transpired behind the scenes also supports the conclusion that state banks were overwhelmingly supportive of the Bank of the United States; moreover, he finds that the support was strongest among banks in the western states of Ohio and Kentucky (Henry Clay's home state) and the southern states of North Carolina, Louisiana, and Alabama. This support was not surprising, since—after the Panic of 1819 and the ensuing conflicts—the Bank had managed to expand its loans in those areas of the country. In fact, in 1827 about 60 percent of the Bank's total loans and 70 percent of its notes were issued in these two regions. See Wilburn 1957, 48–50.

69. McGrane 1919, 93, 172.

70. Jackson apparently revealed as much in a private meeting with Biddle. See Catterall 1902, 183–184; McGrane 1919, 93.

71. Woolley and Peters n.d.

72. Hoffmann argues that Jackson's alternative bank plan was part of a long-term strategy to completely separate government from banking, based on the theories of the economist William Gouge, who worked in the Treasury Department. But, as she also observes, Jackson's contemporaries did not really interpret the plan that way: influential bankers and policy makers viewed it as the government trying to control banking completely (Hoffmann 2001, 61–65). And it was this interpretation by contemporaneously influential actors, irrespective of what later analysts might theorize as Jackson's ulterior or real motives, that decisively affected outcomes. This was, in turn, because any policy change—even short-term, and whatever its ultimate putative goal—had major distributional implications for influential actors. Again, the problem with Hoffmann's argument is that though it accounts

for Jackson's motivations, it does not succeed in explaining the eventual outcomes, since it ignores the environment (strategic and institutional) in which the president was operating. The environment delimited policy possibilities irrespective of Jackson's views and banking theories.

73. McGrane 1919, 91–92, 97.

74. *Report No. 283*, 22nd Cong., 1st sess., 1832. For "Views of the Minority," see ibid., 57.

75. Woolley and Peters n.d.

76. He probably realized this prior to his second address. See Catterall 1902, 208; McGrane 1919, 103–104.

77. McGrane 1919, 196.

78. Some of the banks hesitated initially. See Catterall 1902, 291.

79. Ibid., 296.

80. This account is garnered from Duane's testimony. He published his version of events in 1838. For the president's reasoning, see Duane 1838, 9. Jackson's various defenses of the state banks can also be found in his letters to Duane, which Duane published as a part of this book. See also ibid., 96–100.

81. For a Senate Finance Committee report opposing the president's moves, see *S. Doc. 72*, 23rd Cong., 1st sess., 1834.

82. Catterall 1902, 329.

83. Ibid., 338.

84. Ibid., 339.

85. Ibid., 347; see also ibid., 340–350.

86. For details, see Timberlake 1960, 109–117; Scheiber 1963, 196–214.

87. Krippner 2011, 145; see also ibid., chap. 2.

88. Gallatin 1881, 44. He estimated that the four years between 1811 and 1815 saw the establishment of at least 120 chartered banks. This was, indeed, quite an increase, considering that the number of banks in 1811 totaled about 88. An increase in the number of bank notes accompanied the increase in banks. By Gallatin's estimates, the circulation of notes increased from about $28,000,000 to almost $46,000,000, while the corresponding increase in specie was from only about $15,500,000 to $17,000,000.

89. Hammond 1957, 453.

Chapter 6

1. Schumpeter 1939, 109–123.

2. Gerschenkron 1962; Cameron 1967, 1972; Sylla 1975.

3. Sylla, Tilly, and Tortella 1999.

4. Acemoglu, Johnson, and Robinson, 2001, 2002, 2005.

5. La Porta, Lopez-de-Silanes, and Shleifer 2008, 307–308, 310–311.

6. Ibid., 299.

7. Ibid., 308.

8. Roe 2006; Roe and Siegel 2009. See also Musacchio and Turner 2013.

9. Roe 2006, 475.

10. Roe and Siegel 2009, 783.

11. Ibid.

12. Ibid., 784.

13. Ibid., 786.

14. Ibid., 790, 791.

15. Ibid, 788–791; Roe 2006, 495–510.

16. Roe 2006, 464.

17. Ibid., 482, 496.

18. Roe and Siegel 2009, 789; Rajan and Zingales 2003.

19. Knight 1992, 41.

20. Such arguments are not uncommon in political science or sociology. See, e.g., Waldner 1999; Chibber 2003.

21. For a similar, though not identical, critique, see Chang 2011. Note that the approach of simply listing possible variables is amenable to such statistical testing. For instance, the legal origins literature controls for some of the factors that Roe 2006 mentions as relevant, such as left party dominance. See La Porta, Lopez-de-Silanes, and Shleifer 2008, 311–315; Beck, Demirgüç-Kunt, and Levine 2003a, 2003b.

22. Roe and Siegel 2009, 793–796; Roe 2006, 513–515.

23. Roe 2006, 513.

24. Roe claims the same for his argument about the relevance of the effects of World War II. As he puts it, "Postwar political forces make a difference, but the difference is conditional on the nation's being one of the world's richer democracies" (ibid., 514).

25. This is the only nontautological way of interpreting Roe's comparability criterion: that some countries are rich while others are poor cannot be the relevant basis for creating like or unlike categories, because doing this simply ends up begging the question (all the more because the legal origins of institutions are ultimately supposed to affect the level of economic development).

26. Roe and Siegel 2009, 783; Chang 2002, 2011.

27. Rajan and Zingales 2003.

28. La Porta, Lopez-de-Silanes, and Shleifer 2008, 317.

29. Ibid., 318.

30. Roe 2006, 509.

31. Ibid., 508.

32. Knight 1992.

33. Roe 2006, 509.

34. La Porta, Lopez-de-Silanes, and Shleifer 2008, 304.

35. Beck, Demirgüç-Kunt, and Levine 2003a, 360. One might inquire here about the reasons behind these superior French ratiocinative abilities.

36. Arguments based on culture, for instance, are not necessarily consistent—pending a theoretical effort to reconcile them—with factors that imply self-inter-

ested, rational actors' calculation of the distributional consequences of rules and regulations. Yet Roe and Siegel (2009, 787) cite both as part of a long list under the heading "Political Economy."

37. This is especially true, since there is no *a priori* reason to believe that all developing countries must be alike in certain ways and must therefore be compared with only one another. As I argued above, comparability depends on the theoretical stance one takes.

38. Roe and Siegel 2009, 789.

39. Acemoglu, Johnson, and Robinson 2001, 2002, 2005.

40. See Acemoglu, Johnson, and Robinson 2001, 2002.

41. Mortality rate is asserted as a mechanism in Acemoglu, Johnson, and Robinson 2001, while prosperity appears as a factor in Acemoglu, Johnson, and Robinson 2002.

42. Acemoglu, Johnson, and Robinson 2001, 1370.

43. Ibid., 1375.

44. Ibid., 1376.

45. Ibid., 1376–1377.

46. Acemoglu, Johnson, and Robinson 2002, 1235.

47. They also note this in their 2002 article (see ibid., 1268–1269).

48. Beck, Demirgüç-Kunt, and Levine 2003b.

49. See the section in Chapter 4 titled "The United States and India: Some Observations."

50. Acemoglu, Johnson, and Robinson 2001. The democracy index is not used in Acemoglu, Johnson, and Robinson 2002.

51. Acemoglu, Johnson, and Robinson 2001, 2002, 2005.

52. Chang 2002, 2011.

References

Acemoglu, D., S. Johnson, and J. A. Robinson. 2001. "The Colonial Origins of Comparative Development: An Empirical Investigation." *American Economic Review* 91 (5): 1369–1401.

———. 2002. "Reversal of Fortune: Geography and Institutions in the Making of the Modern World Income Distribution." *Quarterly Journal of Economics* 117 (4): 1231–1294.

———. 2005. "Institutions as a Fundamental Cause of Long-Run Growth." In *Handbook of Economic Growth*, ed. P. Aghion and S. N. Durlauf, vol. 1A, 386–472. Elsevier, Amsterdam.

Alvord, C. W. 1916. "Virginia and the West: An Interpretation." *Mississippi Valley Historical Review* 3 (1): 19–38.

Andrew A. P. 1901. "Indian Currency Problems of the Last Decade." *Quarterly Journal of Economics* 15 (4): 483–516.

Atwater, J. 1811. "Considerations on the Approaching Dissolution of the United States Bank." *American Mercury* 27, no. 1384 (January 10): 1–2.

Bagchi, A. K. 1985. "Transition from Indian to British Indian Systems of Money and Banking, 1800–1850." *Modern Asian Studies* 19 (3): 501–519.

———. 1987. *The Evolution of the State Bank of India: The Roots, 1806–1876.* Part 1, *The Early Years, 1806–1860.* Bombay: Oxford University Press.

Banerji, A. 1995. *Finances in the Early Raj: Investments and the External Sector.* New Delhi: Sage.

"Bank of the United States." 1810a. *New Hampshire Patriot* 2, no. 86 (December 4).

"Bank of the United States." 1810b. *Newport Mercury* 50, no. 2541 (December 29).

"Bank of the United States." 1811a. *American Advocate* 1, no. 52 (January 16): 2.

"The Bank of the United States." 1811b. *Berkshire Reporter*, January 12.

Bayly, C. A. 1973. "Patrons and Politics in Northern India." *Modern Asian Studies* 7 (3): 349–388.

———. 1983. *Rulers, Townsmen and Bazaars: North Indian Society in the Age of British Expansion, 1770–1870.* Delhi: Oxford University Press.

———. 2000. "Ireland, India and the Empire: 1780–1914." *Transactions of the Royal Historical Society* 6 (10): 377–397.

Beard, C. A. (1913) 1935. *An Economic Interpretation of the Constitution of the United States.* Reprint, New York: Macmillan.

Beck, T., A. Demirgüç-Kunt, and R. Levine. 2003a. "Law and Finance: Why Does Legal Origin Matter?" *Journal of Comparative Economics* 31 (4): 653–675.

———. 2003b. "Law, Endowments, and Finance." *Journal of Financial Economics* 70 (2): 137–181.

Becker, C. L. 1901. "Nominations in Colonial New York." *American Historical Review* 6 (2): 260–275.

———. 1909. *History of Political Parties in the Province of New York, 1760–1776.* Madison: University of Wisconsin Press.

Bernier, F. 1891. *Travels in the Mogul Empire, 1656–1668.* Trans. Archibald Constable. London: Archibald Constable.

Bezanson, A. 1951. *Prices and Inflation during the American Revolution: Pennsylvania, 1750–1790.* Philadelphia: University of Pennsylvania Press.

Bhattacharya, S. 1969. *The East India Company and the Economy of Bengal from 1704 to 1740.* Calcutta: Firma K. L. Mukhopadhyay.

———. 1983. "Eastern India." In *The Cambridge Economic History of India*, vol. 2, *c. 1757–1970*, ed. D. Kumar, 86–177. Cambridge: Cambridge University Press.

Blodget, S. 1804. "Observations on the New Bank of Potomac & c." *National Intelligencer and Washington Advertiser*, September 19, 1.

Bowen, H. V. 2005. *The Business of Empire: The East India Company and Imperial Britain, 1756–1833.* Cambridge: Cambridge University Press.

Bowman, J. 2006. *Capitalist Collective Action: Competition, Cooperation and Conflict in the Coal Industry.* New York: Cambridge University Press.

Box-Steffensmeier, J., Henry E. Brady, and David Collier, eds. 2008. *The Oxford Handbook of Political Methodology.* New York: Oxford University Press.

Brock, L. V. 1975. *The Currency of the American Colonies, 1700–1764: A Study in Colonial Finance and Imperial Relations.* New York: Arno Press.

Brown, K. L. 1942. "Stephen Girard, Promoter of the Second Bank of the United States." *Journal of Economic History* 2 (2): 125–148.

Brown, R. E. 1952. "Democracy in Colonial Massachusetts." *New England Quarterly* 25 (3): 291–313.

———. 1953. "Restriction of Representation in Colonial Massachusetts." *Mississippi Valley Historical Review* 40 (3): 463–476.

Bruchey, S. 1970. "Alexander Hamilton and the State Banks, 1789 to 1795." *William and Mary Quarterly* 27 (3): 347–378.

Cameron, R. 1967. *Banking in the Early Stages of Industrialization: A Study in Comparative Economic History.* New York: Oxford University Press.

———, ed. 1972. *Banking and Economic Development: Some Lessons of History.* New York: Oxford University Press.

Carey, M. 1810. "Desultory Reflections upon the Ruinous Consequences of a Non-renewal of the Charter of the Bank of the United States." *Commercial Advertiser* (New York), May 12, 2.

Carpenter, D. 2008. "Institutional Strangulation: Bureaucratic Politics and Financial Reform in the Obama Administration." *Perspectives on Politics* 8 (3): 825–846.

Catterall, R.C.H. 1902. *The Second Bank of the United States.* Chicago: University of Chicago Press.

Chandavarkar, A. G. 1983. "Money and Credit, 1858–1947." In Kumar, *Cambridge Economic History of India,* 762–803.

Chang, H. J. 2002. *Kicking Away the Ladder: Development Strategy in Historical Perspective.* London: Anthem.

———. 2011. "Institutions and Economic Development: Theory, Policy and History." *Journal of Institutional Economics* 7 (4): 473–498.

Chatterjee, A. 2013. "Ontology, Epistemology, and Multi-method Research in Political Science." *Philosophy of the Social Sciences* 43 (1): 73–99.

Chatterjee, K. 1996. *Merchants, Politics, and Society in Early Modern India, Bihar: 1733–1820.* Leiden, Netherlands: E. J. Brill.

Chaudhuri, K. N. 1978. *The Trading World of Asia and the English East India Company, 1660–1760.* Cambridge: Cambridge University Press.

———. 1985. *Trade and Civilization in the Indian Ocean: An Economic History from the Rise of Islam to 1750.* Cambridge: Cambridge University Press.

Chaudhuri, S. 1975. *Trade and Commercial Organization in Bengal, 1650–1720.* Calcutta: Firma K. L. Mukhopadhyay.

Chaudhury, S. 1988. "Merchants, Companies and Rulers: Bengal in the Eighteenth Century." *Journal of the Economic and Social History of the Orient* 31 (1): 74–109.

Chibber, V. 2003. *Locked in Place: State Building and Late Industrialization in India.* Princeton, NJ: Princeton University Press.

Clark, M. S., and D. A. Hall. 1832. *Legislative and Documentary History of the Bank of the United States including the Original Bank of North America.* Washington, DC: Gales and Seaton.

Cohen, H. 1971. *Business and Politics in America from the Age of Jackson to the Civil War.* Westport, CT: Greenwood.

Cohn, B. S. 1960. "The Initial British Impact on India: A Case Study of the Benares Region." *Journal of Asian Studies* 19 (4): 418–431.

A Commercial Capitalist of New York. 1810. "On the Subject of the Bank of the United States." *Weekly Aurora,* no. 25 (December 4): 2.

Common Sense. 1811. "Bank of the United States." *Northern Centinel,* January 17.

Corrector. 1810a. "Bank of the United States." *Old Colony Gazette* 3, no. 9 (December 14): 1.

———. 1810b. "Bank of the United States." *Weekly Aurora,* no. 25 (December 4): 2.

Corwin, E. S. 1915. "The French Objective in the American Revolution." *American Historical Review* 21 (1): 33–61.

Countryman, E. 1981. *A People in Revolution: The American Revolution and Political Society in New York, 1760–1790.* New York: W. W. Norton.

Cowen, D. J. 2000a. "The First Bank of the United States and the Securities Market Crash of 1792." *Journal of Economic History* 60 (4): 1041–1060.

———. 2000b. *The Origins and Economic Impact of the First Bank of the United States, 1791–1797.* New York: Garland.

"Crowninshield on Banks." 1806. *United States Gazette* 30, no. 4478 (December 30).

———. 1807. *Boston Gazette* 71, no. 21 (January 8): 2.

Curtis, T. D. 1972. "Land Policy: Pre-condition for the Success of the American Revolution." *American Journal of Economics and Sociology* 31: 2.

Das Gupta, A. 1982. "Indian Merchants and the Trade in the Indian Ocean." In *The Cambridge Economic History of India*, vol. 1, *c. 1200-c. 1750*, ed. Tapan Raychaudhuri and Irfan Habib, 407–433. Cambridge: Cambridge University Press.

Deyell, J. S. 1987. "The Development of Akbar's Currency System and Monetary Integration of the Conquered Kingdoms." In *The Imperial Monetary System of Mughal India*, ed. J. F. Richards, 13–67. Delhi: Oxford University Press.

Dickson, P.G.M. 1967. *The Financial Revolution in England: A Study in the Development of Public Credit, 1688–1756.* New York: St. Martin's Press.

Doerflinger, T. M. 1983. "Philadelphia Merchants and the Logic of Moderation, 1760–1775." *William and Mary Quarterly* 40 (2): 197–226.

———. 1986. *A Vigorous Spirit of Enterprise: Merchants and Economic Development in Revolutionary Philadelphia.* Chapel Hill: University of North Carolina Press.

Duane, W. J. 1838. *Narrative and Correspondence concerning the Removal of the Deposites, and Occurrences Connected Therewith.* Philadelphia.

Dutt, R. C. 1956. *The Economic History of India in the Victorian Age: From the Accession of Queen Victoria in 1837 to the Commencement of the Twentieth Century.* London: Routledge and Keegan Paul.

East, R. A. 1969. *Business Enterprise in the American Revolutionary Era.* New York: AMS Press.

Egnal, M. 1988. *A Mighty Empire: The Origins of the American Revolution.* Ithaca, NY: Cornell University Press.

Egnal, M., and J. A. Ernst. 1972. "An Economic Interpretation of the American Revolution." *William and Mary Quarterly* 29 (1): 3–32.

Elliot, H. M. 1877. *The History of India as Told by Its Own Historians: The Muhammadan Period.* Vol. 7, ed. John Dowson. London: Trubner.

Emerson, R. 1962. "Power-Dependence Relations." *American Sociological Review* 27 (1): 31–41.

Ernst, J. E. 1973. *Money and Politics in America, 1755–1776: A Study in the Currency Act of 1764 and the Political Economy of Revolution.* Chapel Hill: University of North Carolina Press.

Esteban J. C. 2001. "The British Balance of Payments, 1772–1820: India Transfers and War Finance." *Economic History Review* 54 (1): 58–86.

Evans, E. G. 1962. "Planter Indebtedness and the Coming of the Revolution in Virginia." *William and Mary Quarterly*, 3rd ser., vol. 19 (4): 511–533.

"Extract of a Letter to a Gentleman in Georgetown." 1810. *Northern Whig* 2, no. 52 (December 28).

Fazl, A. (1590?) 1891. *A'in I Akbari*. Vol. 2, trans. H. S. Jarrett. Calcutta: Asiatic Society of Bengal.

Ferguson, E. J. 1961. *The Power of the Purse: A History of American Public Finance, 1776–1790*. Chapel Hill: University of North Carolina Press.

Ferguson, T. 1995. *Golden Rule: The Investment Theory of Party Competition and the Logic of Money-Driven Political Systems*. Chicago: University of Chicago Press.

Fifth Report from the Committee of Secrecy Appointed by the House of Commons Assembled at Westminster in the Sixth Session of the Thirteenth Parliament of Great Britain to Enquire into the State of the East India Company. 1773. London.

Fligstein, N. 2002. *The Architecture of Markets: An Economic Sociology of Twenty-First-Century Capitalist Societies*. Princeton, NJ: Princeton University Press.

Furber, H., ed. 1933. *The Private Record of an Indian Governor-Generalship: The Correspondence of Sir John Shore, Governor General, with Henry Dundas, President of the Board of Control, 1793–1798*. Cambridge, MA: Harvard University Press.

———. 1948. *John Company at Work: A Study of European Expansion in India in the Late Eighteenth Century*. Cambridge, MA: Harvard University Press.

Gallatin, A. 1881. *Considerations on the Currency and Banking System of the United States*. Philadelphia: Carey and Lea.

Gerschenkron, A. 1962. *Economic Backwardness in Historical Perspective*. Cambridge: Belknap.

Goldsmith, R. W. 1983. *The Financial Development of India, 1860–1977*. New Haven, CT: Yale University Press.

Grant, J. 1791. An *Inquiry into the Nature of Zemindary Tenures in the Landed Property of Bengal, &c. with an Appendix*. London.

Greene, J. P. 1961. "The Role of Lower Houses of Assembly in Eighteenth-Century Politics." *Journal of Southern History* 27 (4): 451–474.

Greene, J. P., and R. E. Jellison. 1961. "The Currency Act of 1964 in Imperial-Colonial Relations, 1764–1776." *William and Mary Quarterly* 18 (4): 485–518.

Haber, S. 2008. "Political Institutions and Financial Development: Evidence from the Political Economy of Banking Regulation in Mexico and the United States." In *Political Institutions and Financial Development*, ed. S. Haber, D. C. North, and B. R. Weingast, 10–59. Stanford, CA: Stanford University Press.

Haber, S., D. C. North, and B. R. Weingast, eds. 2008. *Institutions and Financial Development*. Stanford, CA: Stanford University Press.

Haber, S., A. Razo, and N. Maurer. 2003. *The Politics of Property Rights: Political Instability, Credible Commitments and Economic Growth in Mexico 1876–1928*. New York: Cambridge University Press.

Habib, I. 1964. "Usury in Medieval India." *Comparative Studies in Society and History* 6 (4): 393–419.

——. 1969. "Potentialities of Capitalistic Development in the Economy of Mughal India." *Journal of Economic History* 29 (1): 32–78.

——. 1982a. "Agrarian Economy." In Raychaudhuri and Habib, *The Cambridge Economic History of India*, 48–76.

——. 1982b. "The Monetary System and Prices." In Raychaudhuri and Habib, *The Cambridge Economic History of India*, 360–381.

Hammond, B. 1957. *Banks and Politics in America: From Revolution to the Civil War.* Princeton, NJ: Princeton University Press.

Handlin, O., and M. F. Handlin. 1947. "Revolutionary Economic Policy in Massachusetts." *William and Mary Quarterly*, 3rd ser., vol. 4 (1): 3–26.

Hardin, R. 1997. *One for All: The Logic of Group Conflict.* Princeton, NJ: Princeton University Press.

Harlow, R. V. 1929. "Aspects of Revolutionary Finance, 1775–1783." *American Historical Review* 35 (1): 46–68.

Harrell, I. H. 1925. "Some Neglected Phases of the Revolution in Virginia." *William and Mary Quarterly*, 2nd ser., vol. 5 (3): 159–170.

Harrington, V. D. 1964. *The New York Merchant on the Eve of the Revolution.* Gloucester, MA: Peter Smith.

Hartz, L. 1948. *Economic Policy and Democratic Thought: Pennsylvania, 1776–1860.* Cambridge, MA: Harvard University Press.

Hill, S. C., ed. (1905) 1968. *Bengal in 1756–1757: A Selection of Public and Private Papers Dealing with the Affairs of the British in Bengal during the Reign of Siraj-Uddaula.* 3 vols. Reprint, New York: AMS Press.

Hoffmann, S. 2001. *Politics and Banking: Ideas, Public Policy, and the Creation of Financial Institutions.* Baltimore: Johns Hopkins University Press.

Holdsworth, J. T., and D. R. Dewey. 1910. *The First and the Second Banks of the United States.* Washington, DC: U.S. Government Printing Office.

Hurd, J. M. 1983. "Irrigation and Railways." In Kumar, *Cambridge Economic History of India*, 737–761.

Ingram, E., ed. 1970. *Two Views of British India: The Private Correspondence of Mr. Dundas and Lord Wellesley.* Bath, UK: Adams and Dart.

Journals of the Continental Congress. 1774–1779. 34 vols.

Keynes, J. M. 1913. *Indian Currency and Finance.* London: Macmillan.

Khan, G. H. 1789. *Seir Mutaqharin, or A View of Modern Times.* Vol. 1. Calcutta: James White.

Kinley, D. 1893. *The History, Organization and Influence of the Independent Treasury of the United States.* New York: Thomas Y. Crowell.

Knight, J. 1992. *Institutions and Social Conflict.* New York: Cambridge University Press.

Konkle, B. A. 1937. *Thomas Willing and the First American Financial System.* Philadelphia: University of Pennsylvania Press.

Krippner, G. R. 2011. *Capitalizing on Crisis: The Political Origins of the Rise of Finance.* Cambridge, MA: Harvard University Press.

Kumar, D. 1983. "The Fiscal System." In Kumar, *The Cambridge Economic History of India*, 905–944.

Lamoreaux, N. R. 1996. *Insider Lending: Banks, Personal Connections, and Economic Development in Industrial New England.* New York: Cambridge University Press.

La Porta, R., F. Lopez-de-Silanes, and A. Shleifer. 2008. "The Economic Consequences of Legal Origins." *Journal of Economic Literature* 46 (2): 285–332.

Leder, L. H., and V. P. Carosso. 1956. "Robert Livingston (1654–1728): Businessman of Colonial New York." *Business History Review* 30 (1): 18–45.

Leonard, J. D. 1954. "Elections in Colonial Pennsylvania." *William and Mary Quarterly* 11 (3): 385–401.

Lester, R. A. 1938. "Currency Issues to Overcome Depression in Pennsylvania, 1723 and 1729." *Journal of Political Economy* 46 (3): 324–375.

———. 1939. "Currency Issues to Overcome Depression in Delaware, New Jersey, New York, and Maryland." *Journal of Political Economy* 47 (2): 182–217.

Levermore, C. H. 1896. "The Whigs of Colonial New York." *American Historical Review* 1 (2): 238–250.

Levy, J. S. 2008. "Counterfactuals and Case Studies." In *The Oxford Handbook of Political Methodology,* ed. J. Box-Steffensmeier, Henry E. Brady, and David Collier, 627–644. New York: Oxford University Press.

Lewis, D. 1993. "Causation." In *Causation,* ed. Ernest Sosa and Michael Tooley, 193–204. New York: Oxford University Press.

Lomazoff, E. 2012. "Turning (into) 'the Great Regulating Wheel': The Conversion of the Bank of the United States, 1791–1811." *Studies in American Political Development* 26 (1): 1–23.

Macaulay, T. 1914. *The History of England.* Vol. 5. London.

Mahoney, J., and K. Thelen. 2010. *Explaining Institutional Change: Ambiguity, Agency and Power.* Cambridge: Cambridge University Press.

Main, J. T. 1961. *The Antifederalists: Critics of the Constitution, 1781–1788.* New York: W. W. Norton.

———. 1963. *Rebel versus Tory: The Crisis of the Revolution, 1773–1776.* Chicago: Rand McNally.

Mallick, B. S. 1991. *Money, Banking and Trade in Mughal India: Currency, Indigenous Fiscal Practices and the English Trade in 17th Century Gujarat and Bengal.* Delhi: Rawat Publications.

Manucci, N. 1907. *Storia do Mogor or Mogul India, 1653–1708.* Vol. 2, trans. William Irvine. London: John Murray.

Marshall, P. J. 1976. *East Indian Fortunes: The British in Bengal in the Eighteenth Century.* Oxford: Clarendon Press.

———. 1987. *Bengal: The British Bridgehead, Eastern India 1740–1828.* The New Cambridge History of India. Cambridge: Cambridge University Press.

Martin, M. H. 1987. "The Reforms of the Sixteenth Century and Akbar's Administration: Metrological and Monetary Considerations." In Richards, *The Imperial Monetary System of Mughal India*, 68–99.

Mason, B. 1966. "Entrepreneurial Activity in New York during the American Revolution." *Business History Review* 40 (2): 190–212.

McCusker, J. J. 1972. "Sources of Investment Capital in the Colonial Philadelphia Shipping Industry." *Journal of Economic History* 32 (1): 146–157.

McGrane, R. C., ed. 1919. *The Correspondence of Nicholas Biddle Dealing with National Affairs.* Boston: Houghton Mifflin.

McGuire, R. A. 2003. *To Form a More Perfect Union: A New Economic Interpretation of the United States Constitution.* New York: Oxford University Press.

Mihm, S. 2007. *A Nation of Counterfeiters: Capitalists, Con Men, and the Making of the United States.* Cambridge, MA: Harvard University Press.

Mitra, D. B. 1991. *Monetary System in the Bengal Presidency, 1757–1835.* Calcutta: K. P. Bagchi.

Moe, T. 2005. "Power and Political Institutions." *Perspectives on Politics* 3 (2): 215–233.

"More Lies and General Smith." 1810. *Federal Republican and Commercial Gazette* 1, no. 150 (March 29): 2.

Musacchio, A., and J. D. Turner. 2013. "Does the Law and Finance Hypothesis Pass the Test of History?" *Business History* 55 (4): 524–542.

Newcomb, B. H. 1966. "Effects of the Stamp Act on Colonial Pennsylvania Politics." *William and Mary Quarterly* 23 (2): 257–272.

North, D. C. 1981. *Structure and Change in Economic History.* New York: W. W. Norton.

———. 1990. *Institutions, Institutional Change, and Economic Performance.* New York: Cambridge University Press.

North, D. C., and R. P. Thomas. 1976. *The Rise of the Western World.* New York: Cambridge University Press.

North, D. C., J. J. Wallis, and B. R. Weingast. 2009. *Violence and Social Orders: A Conceptual Framework for Interpreting Recorded Human History.* New York: Cambridge University Press.

North, D. C., and B. R. Weingast. 1989. "Constitutions and Commitment: The Evolution of Institutions Governing Public Choice in Seventeenth-Century England." *Journal of Economic History* 49 (4): 803–832.

Oaks, R. F. 1970. *Philadelphia Merchants and the American Revolution, 1765–1776.* Ph.D. diss., University of Southern California.

———. 1977. "Philadelphia Merchants and the Origins of American Independence." *Proceedings of the American Philosophical Society* 121 (6): 407–436.

The Papers of James A. Bayard. 1913. In *The Annual Report of the American Historical Association for the Year 1913.* Vol. 2. Washington, DC.

Pearson, M. N. 1976. *Merchants and Rulers in Gujarat: The Response to the Portuguese in the Sixteenth Century.* Berkeley: University of California Press.

Perkins, E. J. 1994. *American Public Finance and Financial Services, 1700–1815.* Columbus: Ohio State University Press.

Polanyi, K. 1957. *The Great Transformation: The Political and Economic Origins of Our Time.* Boston: Beacon Press.

Rajan, R. G., and L. Zingales. 2003. "The Great Reversals: The Politics of Financial Development in the Twentieth Century." *Journal of Financial Economics* 69 (1): 5–50.

Ray, R. K. 1992. *Entrepreneurship and Industry in India, 1800–1947*. Delhi: Oxford University Press.

———, ed. 2003. *The Felt Community: Commonalty and Mentality before the Emergence of Indian Nationalism.* Delhi: Oxford University Press.

Raychaudhuri T. 1982. "The Mughal Empire." In Raychaudhuri and Habib, *The Cambridge Economic History of India*, 172–193.

Redlich, F. 1968. *The Molding of American Banking: Men and Ideas.* Parts 1 and 2. New York: Johnson Reprint.

Richards, J. F. 1981. "Mughal State Finance and the Premodern World Economy." *Comparative Studies in Society and History* 23 (2): 285–308.

———. 1987. "Introduction." In Richards, *The Imperial Monetary System of Mughal India*, 1–12.

Roe, M. J. 2006. "Legal Origins, Politics, and Modern Stock Markets." *Harvard Law Review* 120 (2): 460–527.

Roe, M. J., and J. I. Siegel. 2009. "Finance and Politics: A Review Essay Based on Kenneth Dam's Analysis of Legal Traditions in *The Law-Growth Nexus.*" *Journal of Economic Literature* 47 (3): 781–800.

Russell, B. 1932. *The Conquest of Happiness.* London: George Allen and Unwin.

Ryerson, R. A. 1974. "Political Mobilization and the American Revolution: The Resistance Movement in Philadelphia, 1765 to 1776." *William and Mary Quarterly* 31 (4): 561–588.

Schattschneider, E. E. 1935. *Politics, Pressures, and the Tariff.* New York: Prentice Hall.

Scheiber, H. N. 1963. "The Pet Banks in Jacksonian Politics and Finance, 1833–1841." *Journal of Economic History* 23 (2): 196–214.

Schlesinger, A. M. (1913) 1957. *The Colonial Merchants and the American Revolution, 1763–1776.* Reprint, New York: Fredrick Unger.

Schlesinger, A. M., Jr. (1945) 1971. *The Age of Jackson.* Reprint, Old Saybrook, CT: Konecky and Konecky.

Schumpeter, J. A. 1939. *Business Cycles: A Theoretical, Historical and Statistical Analysis of the Capitalist Process.* Vol. 1. New York: McGraw-Hill.

Schwartz, A. J. 1947. "The Beginning of Competitive Banking in Philadelphia, 1782–1809." *Journal of Political Economy* 55 (5): 417–431.

Sen, A. K. 1992. "The Pattern of British Enterprise in India 1854–1914: A Causal Analysis." In *Entrepreneurship and Industry in India, 1800–1947*, ed. R. K. Ray. Delhi: Oxford University Press.

Shepherd, J. F., and G. M. Walton. 1972. "Trade, Distribution, and Economic Growth in Colonial America." *Journal of Economic History* 32 (1): 128–145.

Sheridan, R. B. 1960. "The British Credit Crisis of 1772 and the American Colonies." *Journal of Economic History* 20 (2): 161–186.

Singh, D. 1974. "The Role of Mahajans in the Rural Economy in Eastern Rajasthan during the 18th Century." *Social Scientist* 2 (10): 20–31.

Sinha, J. C. 1925. "Economic Theorists among the Servants of John Company (1766–1806)." *Economic Journal* 35 (137): 47–59.

Sinha, N. K. 1961. *The Economic History of Bengal: From Plassey to the Permanent Settlement.* Vol. 1. Calcutta: Firma K. L. Mukhopadhyay.

———. 1962. *The Economic History of Bengal: From Plassey to the Permanent Settlement.* Vol. 2. Calcutta: Firma K. L. Mukhopadhyay.

Smelser N., and R. Swedberg, eds. 1994. *The Handbook of Economic Sociology.* Princeton, NJ: Princeton University Press.

Smith, B. D. 1985. "American Colonial Monetary Regimes: The Failure of the Quantity Theory and Some Evidence in Favor of an Alternative View." *Canadian Journal of Economics* 18 (3): 531–565.

Smith, W. R. 1909. "Sectionalism in Pennsylvania during the Revolution." *Political Science Quarterly* 24 (2): 208–235.

Stasavage, D. 2002. "Credible Commitment in Early Modern Europe: North and Weingast Revisited." *Journal of Law, Economics, and Organization* 18 (1): 155–186.

———. 2007. "Partisan Politics and Public Debt: The Importance of the 'Whig Supremacy' for Britain's Financial Revolution." *European Review of Economic History* 11 (1): 123–153.

Steinmo, S. 2008. "What Is Historical Institutionalism?" In *Approaches and Methodologies in the Social Sciences*, ed. D. Della Porta and M. Keating, 118–138. Cambridge: Cambridge University Press.

Steuart J. 1772. *The Principles of Money Applied to the Present State of the Coin of Bengal: Being an Inquiry into the Methods to Be Used for Correcting the Defects of the Present Currency; for Stopping the Drains Which Carry Off the Coin; and for Extending Circulation by Means of Paper Credit.* London.

Studenski, P., and H. E. Kroos. 1952. *Financial History of the United States.* New York: McGraw-Hill.

Subrahmanyam, S. 2001. "Introduction: The Indian Ocean World and Ashin Das Gupta." In *The World of the Indian Ocean Merchant 1500–1800: Collected Essays of Ashin Das Gupta*, by Ashin Das Gupta, 1–22. New Delhi: Oxford University Press.

Subramanian, L. 1996. *Indigenous Capital and Imperial Expansion: Bombay, Surat, and the West Coast.* Bombay: Oxford University Press.

Subramanian, L., and R. K. Ray. 1991. "Merchants and Politics: From the Great Mughals to the East India Company." In *Business and Politics in India: A Historical Perspective,* ed. D. Tripathi. Delhi: Manohar.

Swedberg, R., and O. Agevall. 2005. *The Max Weber Dictionary: Key Words and Central Concepts.* Stanford, CA: Stanford University Press.

Sylla, R. 1975. *The American Capital Market, 1846–1914: A Study of the Effects of Public Policy on Economic Development.* New York: Arno Press.

———. 2000. "Experimental Federalism: The Economics of American Government, 1789–1914." In *The Cambridge Economic History of the United States*, vol. 2, *The Long Nineteenth Century*, ed. Stanley L. Engerman and Robert E. Gallman, 483–542. Cambridge: Cambridge University Press.

Sylla, R., R. Tilly, and G. Tortella, eds. 1999. *The State, the Financial System and Economic Modernization*. Cambridge: Cambridge University Press.

Tate, T. W. 1962. "The Coming of the Revolution in Virginia: Britain's Challenge to Virginia's Ruling Class, 1763–1776." *William and Mary Quarterly*, 3rd ser., vol. 19 (3): 323–343.

Tavernier, J. B. (1676) 1889. *Travels in India*. Vol. 1, trans. V. Ball. London: Macmillan.

Thayer, T. 1953. "The Land Bank System in the American Colonies." *Journal of Economic History* 13 (2): 145–159.

Thelen, K., and S. Steinmo. 1992. "Historical Institutionalism in Comparative Politics." In *Structuring Politics: Historical Institutionalism in Comparative Analysis*, ed. S. Steinmo, K. Thelen, and F. Longstreth, 1–33. Cambridge: Cambridge University Press.

Tiedmann, J. S. 1984. "Communities in the Midst of the American Revolution: Queens County, New York, 1774–1775." *Journal of Social History* 18 (1): 57–78.

———. 1986. "Patriots by Default: Queens County, New York, and the British Army, 1776–1783." *William and Mary Quarterly*, 3rd ser., 43 (1): 35–63.

———. 1988. "A Revolution Foiled: Queens County, New York, 1774–1775." *Journal of American History* 75 (2): 407–444.

Tilly, C. 1992. *Coercion, Capital and the European State, AD 990–1999*. Cambridge, UK: Blackwell.

Timberlake, R. H., Jr. 1960. "The Specie Circular and Distribution of the Surplus." *Journal of Political Economy* 68 (2): 109–117.

Tripathi, A. 1979. *Trade and Finance in the Bengal Presidency, 1793–1833*. Calcutta: Oxford University Press.

Tyler, J. W. 1986. *Smugglers and Patriots: Boston Merchants and the Advent of the American Revolution*. Boston: Northeastern University Press.

Union. 1811. "Bank of the United States." *American Advocate* 1, no. 51 (January 9): 2.

"United States Bank; Excerpt of a Letter to a Gentleman in Georgetown, D.C., Dated Philadelphia, Oct 13 1810." 1810. *Poulson's American Daily Advertiser* 39, no. 10 (December 14): 2.

"U.S. Bank." 1811. *American Mercury* 27, no. 1384 (January 10).

"The U.S. Bank, Again." 1810. *The Enquirer*, December 27, 2–3.

Vansittart, H. (1766) 1976. *A Narrative of the Transactions in Bengal, 1760–1764*. Ed. Anil Chandra Banerjee and Bimal Kanti Ghosh. Reprint, Calcutta: K. P. Bagchi.

Verelst, H. 1772. *A View of the Rise, Progress, and the Present State of the English Government in Bengal: Including a Reply to the Misrepresentations of Mr. Bolts, and Other Writers*. London.

Waldner, D. 1999. *State Building and Late Development.* Ithaca, NY: Cornell University Press.

Walters, R., Jr. 1945. "The Origins of the Second Bank of the United States." *Journal of Political Economy* 53 (2): 115–131.

Warden, G. B. 1964. "The Proprietary Group in Pennsylvania, 1754–1764." *William and Mary Quarterly* 21 (3): 367–389.

Watson, I. B. 1980. *Foundation for Empire: English Private Trade in India, 1659–1760.* New Delhi: Vikas Publications.

Weber, Max. 1946. "The Social Psychology of the World Religions." In *From Max Weber, Essays in Sociology*, ed. H. H Gerth, and C. Wright Mills, 267–301. New York: Oxford University Press.

Wettereau, J. O. 1942. "The Branches of the First Bank of the United States." *Journal of Economic History* 2 (supplement): 66–100.

Wicker, E. 1985. "Colonial Monetary Standards Contrasted: Evidence from the Seven Years' War." *Journal of Economic History* 45 (4): 869–884.

Wilburn, J. A. 1967. *Biddle's Bank: The Crucial Years.* New York: Columbia University Press.

Woolley, J. T., and G. Peters. n.d. *The American Presidency Project* [online]. Santa Barbara: University of California (hosted), Gerhard Peters (database). Available at http://www.presidency.ucsb.edu/ws/?pid=29471.

Wright, R. E. 1999. "Bank Ownership and Lending Patterns in New York and Pennsylvania, 1781–1831." *Business History Review* 73 (1): 40–60.

Young, A. 1987. "Review." *New England Quarterly* 60 (1): 124–127.

Zemsky, R. M. 1969. "Power, Influence, and Status: Leadership Patterns in the Massachusetts Assembly, 1740–1755." *William and Mary Quarterly* 26 (4): 502–520.

Zimmerman, J. J. 1960. "Benjamin Franklin and the Quaker Party, 1755–1756." *William and Mary Quarterly* 17 (3): 292–313.

Index

ABHISHEK CHATTERJEE is an Assistant Professor of Political Science at the University of Montana in Missoula.